SELECTED POEMS

SELECTED POEMS

— * —

FLEUR ADCOCK

for Lewis
with best wishes
Fleur Adcock
1 March 1990

Oxford   Auckland

OXFORD UNIVERSITY PRESS

Oxford University Press, Walton Street, Oxford OX2 6DP

Oxford New York Toronto
Delhi Bombay Calcutta Madras Karachi
Petaling Jaya Singapore Hong Kong Tokyo
Nairobi Dar es Salaam Cape Town
Melbourne Auckland

and associated companies in
Beirut Berlin Ibadan Nicosia

Oxford is a trade mark of Oxford University Press

ISBN 0-19-558100-8

First published 1983
Reprinted 1984, 1986, 1987

Printed in Great Britain by
J. W. Arrowsmith Ltd, Bristol

ACKNOWLEDGEMENTS

Acknowledgements are due to Bloodaxe Books, who published the pamphlet *Below Loughrigg* (1979), and to the editors of the following magazines and collections, in which some of the more recent poems appeared: *Cosmopolitan, Encounter, The Honest Ulsterman, Islands, Landfall, New Poetry 7* (Arts Council), *New Statesman, PN Review, Poetry Book Society Christmas Supplements* (1979 and 1981), *Poetry Durham, Poetry Review, Poetry Wales, Portland Review, Quarto, The Times Literary Supplement, Writing Women.* 'Blue Glass' was broadcast by the BBC.

The author gratefully acknowledges the support of Northern Arts and the Arts Council of Great Britain.

CONTENTS

SELECTED POEMS

EARLY POEMS

NOTE ON PROPERTIUS

Among the Roman love-poets, possession
Is a rare theme. The locked and flower-hung door,
The shivering lover, are allowed. To more
Buoyant moods, the canons of expression
Gave grudging sanction. Do we, then, assume,
Finding Propertius tear-sodden and jealous,
That Cynthia was inexorably callous?
Plenty of moonlight entered that high room
Whose doors had met his Alexandrine battles;
And she, so gay a lutanist, was known
To stitch and doze a night away, alone,
Until the poet tumbled in with apples
For penitence and for her head his wreath,
Brought from a party, of wine-scented roses –
(The garland's aptness lying, one supposes,
Less in the flowers than in the thorns beneath:
Her waking could, he knew, provide his verses
With less idyllic themes.) Onto her bed
He rolled the round fruit, and adorned her head;
Then gently roused her sleeping mouth to curses.
Here the conventions reassert their power:
The apples fall and bruise, the roses wither,
Touched by a sallowed moon. But there were other
Luminous nights – (even the cactus flower
Glows briefly golden, fed by spiny flesh) –
And once, as he acknowledged, all was singing:
The moonlight musical, the darkness clinging,
And she compliant to his every wish.

FLIGHT, WITH MOUNTAINS

(In Memory of David Herron)

1

Tarmac, take-off: metallic words conduct us
Over that substance, black with spilt rain,
To this event. Sealed, we turn and pause.
Engines churn and throb to a climax, then
Up: a hard spurt, and the passionate rise
Levels out for this gradual incline.

There was something of pleasure in that thrust
From earth into ignorant cloud; but here,
Above all tremors of sensation, rest
Replaces motion; secretly we enter
The obscurely gliding current, and encased
In vitreous calm inhabit the high air.

Now I see, beneath the plated wing,
Cloud edges withdrawing their slow foam
From shoreline, rippling hills, and beyond, the long
Crested range of the land's height. I am
Carried too far by this blind rocketing:
Faced with mountains, I remember him

Whose death seems a convention of such a view:
Another one for the mountains. Another one
Who, climbing to stain the high snow
With his shadow, fell, and briefly caught between
Sudden earth and sun, projected below
A flicker of darkness; as, now, this plane.

2

Only air to hold the wings;
Only words to hold the story;
Only a frail web of cells
To hold heat in the body.

Breath bleeds from throat and lungs
Under the last cold fury;
Words wither; meaning fails;
Steel wings grow heavy.

2

3

Headlines announced it, over a double column of type:
The cabled facts, public regret, and a classified list
Of your attainments – degrees, scholarships and positions,
And notable feats of climbing. So the record stands:
No place there for my private annotations. The face
That smiles in some doubt from a fuscous half-tone block
Stirs me hardly more than those I have mistaken
Daily, about the streets, for yours.
                                    I can refer
To my own pictures; and turning first to the easiest,
Least painful, I see Dave the raconteur,
Playing a shoal of listeners on a casual line
Of dry narration. Other images unreel:
Your face in a car, silent, watching the dark road,
Or animated and sunburnt from your hard pleasures
Of snow and rock-face; again, I see you arguing,
Practical and determined, as you draw with awkward puffs
At a rare cigarette.
                    So much, in vivid sequence
Memory gives. And then, before I can turn away,
Imagination adds the last scene: your eyes bruised,
Mouth choked under a murderous weight of snow.

4

'When you reach the top of a mountain, keep on climbing' –
Meaning, we may suppose,
To sketch on space the cool arabesques of birds
In plastic air, or those
Exfoliating arcs, upward and outward,
Of an aeronautic show.
Easier, such a free fall in reverse,
Higher than clogging snow
Or clutching gravity, than the awkward local
Embrace of rocks. And observe
The planets coursing their elliptical race-tracks,
Where each completed curve
Cinctures a new dimension. Mark these patterns.
Mark, too, how the high
Air thins. The top of any mountain
Is a base for the sky.

5

Further by days and oceans than all my flying
You have gone, while here the air insensibly flowing
Over a map of mountains drowns my dumbness.
A turn of the earth away, where a crawling dimness
Waits now to absorb our light, another
Snowscape, named like this one, took you; and neither
Rope, nor crumbling ice, nor your unbelieving
Uncommitted hands could hold you to living.
Wheels turn; the dissolving air rolls over
An arc of thunder. Gone is gone forever.

BEAUTY ABROAD

Carrying still the dewy rose
For which she's bound to payment, Beauty goes
Trembling through the gruesome wood:
Small comfort to her that she's meek and good.
A branch cracks, and the beast appears:
She sees the fangs, the eyes, the bristly ears,
Stifles a scream, and smooths her dress;
But his concern is for his own distress.
He lays his muzzle on her hand,
Says 'Pity me!' and 'Can you understand?
Be kind!' And then goes on to praise
Her pretty features and her gentle ways.
Beauty inclines a modest ear,
Hears what she has decided she should hear,
And with no thought to ask 'What then?'
Follows the creature to his hairy den.
The beast, like any hero, knows
Sweet talk can lead him to *la belle chose*.

KNIFE-PLAY

All my scars are yours. We talk of pledges,
And holding out my hand I show
The faint burn on the palm and the hair-thin
Razor-marks at wrist and elbow:

Self-inflicted, yes; but your tokens –
Made as distraction from a more
Inaccessible pain than could have been
Caused by cigarette or razor –

And these my slightest marks. In all our meetings
You were the man with the long knives,
Piercing the living hopes, cutting connections,
Carving and dissecting motives,

And with an expert eye for dagger-throwing:
A showman's aim. Oh, I could dance
And dodge, as often as not, the whistling blades,
Turning on a brave performance

To empty stands. I leaned upon a hope
That this might prove to have been less
A gladiatorial show, contrived for murder,
Than a formal test of fitness

(Initiation rites are always painful)
To bring me ultimately to your
Regard. Well, in a sense it was; for now
I have found some kind of favour:

You have learnt softness; I, by your example,
Am well-schooled in contempt; and while
You speak of truce I laugh, and to your pleading
Turn a cool and guarded profile.

I have now, you might say, the upper hand:
These knives that bristle in my flesh
Increase my armoury and lessen yours.
I can pull out, whet and polish

Your weapons, and return to the attack,
Well-armed. It is a pretty trick,
But one that offers little consolation.
Such a victory would be Pyrrhic,

Occurring when my strength is almost spent.
No: I would make an end of fighting
And, bleeding as I am from old wounds,
Die like the bee upon a sting.

5

INSTRUCTIONS TO VAMPIRES

I would not have you drain
With your sodden lips the flesh that has fed mine,
And leech his bubbling blood to a decline:
Not that pain;

Nor visit on his mind
That other desiccation, where the wit
Shrivels: so to be humbled is not fit
For his kind.

But use acid or flame,
Secretly, to brand or cauterize;
And on the soft globes of his mortal eyes
Etch my name.

INCIDENT

When you were lying on the white sand,
A rock under your head, and smiling,
(Circled by dead shells), I came to you
And you said, reaching to take my hand,
'Lie down'. So for a time we lay
Warm on the sand, talking and smoking,
Easy; while the grovelling sea behind
Sucked at the rocks and measured the day.
Lightly I fell asleep then, and fell
Into a cavernous dream of falling.
It was all the cave-myths, it was all
The myths of tunnel or tower or well –
Alice's rabbit-hole into the ground,
Or the path of Orpheus: a spiral staircase
To hell, furnished with danger and doubt.
Stumbling, I suddenly woke; and found
Water about me. My hair was wet,
And you were sitting on the grey sand,
Waiting for the lapping tide to take me:
Watching, and lighting a cigarette.

UNEXPECTED VISIT

I have nothing to say about this garden.
I do not want to be here, I can't explain
What happened. I merely opened a usual door
And found this. The rain

Has just stopped, and the gravel paths are trickling
With water. Stone lions, on each side,
Gleam like wet seals, and the green birds
Are stiff with dripping pride.

Not my kind of country. The gracious vistas,
The rose-gardens and terraces, are all wrong –
As comfortless as the weather. But here I am.
I cannot tell how long

I have stood gazing at grass too wet to sit on,
Under a sky so dull I cannot read
The sundial, staring along the curving walks
And wondering where they lead;

Not really hoping, though, to be enlightened.
It must be morning, I think, but there is no
Horizon behind the trees, no sun as clock
Or compass. I shall go

And find, somewhere among the formal hedges
Or hidden behind a trellis, a toolshed. There
I can sit on a box and wait. Whatever happens
May happen anywhere,

And better, perhaps, among the rakes and flowerpots
And sacks of bulbs than under this pallid sky:
Having chosen nothing else, I can at least
Choose to be warm and dry.

FOR ANDREW

'Will I die?' you ask. And so I enter on
The dutiful exposition of that which you
Would rather not know, and I rather not tell you.
To soften my 'Yes' I offer compensations –
Age and fulfilment ('It's so far away;
You will have children and grandchildren by then')
And indifference ('By then you will not care').
No need: you cannot believe me, convinced
That if you always eat plenty of vegetables
And are careful crossing the street you will live for ever.
And so we close the subject, with much unsaid –
This, for instance: Though you and I may die
Tomorrow or next year, and nothing remain
Of our stock, of the unique, preciously-hoarded
Inimitable genes we carry in us,
It is possible that for many generations
There will exist, sprung from whatever seeds,
Children straight-limbed, with clear enquiring voices,
Bright-eyed as you. Or so I like to think:
Sharing in this your childish optimism.

FOR A FIVE-YEAR-OLD

A snail is climbing up the window-sill
Into your room, after a night of rain.
You call me in to see, and I explain
That it would be unkind to leave it there:
It might crawl to the floor; we must take care
That no one squashes it. You understand,
And carry it outside, with careful hand,
To eat a daffodil.

I see, then, that a kind of faith prevails:
Your gentleness is moulded still by words
From me, who have trapped mice and shot wild birds,
From me, who drowned your kittens, who betrayed
Your closest relatives, and who purveyed
The harshest kind of truth to many another.
But that is how things are: I am your mother,
And we are kind to snails.

8

COMMENT

The four-year-old believes he likes
Vermouth; the cat eats cheese;
And you and I, though scarcely more
Convincingly than these,
Walk in the gardens, hand in hand,
Beneath the summer trees.

MISS HAMILTON IN LONDON

It would not be true to say she was doing nothing:
She visited several bookshops, spent an hour
In the Victoria and Albert Museum (Indian section),
And walked carefully through the streets of Kensington
Carrying five mushrooms in a paper bag,
A tin of black pepper, a literary magazine,
And enough money to pay the rent for two weeks.
The sky was cloudy, leaves lay on the pavements.

Nor did she lack human contacts: she spoke
To three shop-assistants and a newsvendor,
And returned the 'Goodnight' of a museum attendant.
Arriving home, she wrote a letter to someone
In Canada, as it might be, or in New Zealand,
Listened to the news as she cooked her meal,
And conversed for five minutes with the landlady.
The air was damp with the mist of late autumn.

A full day, and not unrewarding.
Night fell at the usual seasonal hour.
She drew the curtains, switched on the electric fire,
Washed her hair and read until it was dry,
Then went to bed; where, for the hours of darkness,
She lay pierced by thirty black spears
And felt her limbs numb, her eyes burning,
And dark rust carried along her blood.

THE MAN WHO X-RAYED AN ORANGE

Viewed from the top, he said, it was like a wheel,
The paper-thin spokes raying out from the hub
To the half-transparent circumference of rind,
With small dark ellipses suspended between.
He could see the wood of the table-top through it.
Then he knelt, and with his eye at orange-level
Saw it as the globe, its pithy core
Upright from pole to flattened pole. Next,
Its levitation: sustained (or so he told us)
By a week's diet of nothing but rice-water
He had developed powers, drawing upon which
He raised it to a height of about two feet
Above the table, with never a finger near it.
That was all. It descended, gradually opaque,
To rest; while he sat giddy and shivering.
(He shivered telling it.) But surely, we asked,
(And still none of us mentioned self-hypnosis
Or hallucinations caused by lack of food),
Surely triumphant too? Not quite, he said,
With his little crooked smile. It was not enough:
He should have been able to summon up,
Created out of what he had newly learnt,
A perfectly imaginary orange, complete
In every detail; whereupon the real orange
Would have vanished. Then came explanations
And his talk of mysticism, occult physics,
Alchemy, the Qabalah – all his hobby-horses.
If there was failure, it was only here
In the talking. For surely he had lacked nothing,
Neither power nor insight nor imagination,
When he knelt alone in his room, seeing before him
Suspended in the air that golden globe,
Visible and transparent, light-filled:
His only fruit from the Tree of Life.

COMPOSITION FOR WORDS AND PAINT

This darkness has a quality
That poses us in shapes and textures,
One plane behind another,
Flatness in depth.

Your face; a fur of hair; a striped
Curtain behind, and to one side cushions;
Nothing recedes, all lies extended.
I sink upon your image.

I see a soft metallic glint,
A tinsel weave behind the canvas,
Aluminium and bronze beneath the ochre.
There is more in this than we know.

I can imagine drawn around you
A white line, in delicate brush-strokes:
Emphasis; but you do not need it.
You have completeness.

I am not measuring your gestures;
(I have seen you measure those of others,
Know a mind by a hand's trajectory,
The curve of a lip).

But you move, and I move towards you,
Draw back your head, and I advance.
I am fixed to the focus of your eyes.
I share your orbit.

Now I discover things about you:
Your thin wrists, a tooth missing;
And how I melt and burn before you.
I have known you always.

The greyness from the long windows
Reduces visual depth; but tactile
Reality defies half-darkness.
My hands prove you solid.

You draw me down upon your body,
Hard arms behind my head.
Darkness and soft colours blur.
We have swallowed the light.

Now I dissolve you in my mouth,
Catch in the corners of my throat
The sly taste of your love, sliding
Into me, singing;

Just as the birds have started singing.
Let them come flying through the windows
With chains of opals around their necks.
We are expecting them.

REGRESSION

All the flowers have gone back into the ground.
We fell on them, and they did not lie
Crushed and crumpled, waiting to die
On the earth's surface. No: they suddenly wound

The film of their growth backwards. We saw them shrink
From blossom to bud to tiny shoot,
Down from the stem and up from the root.
Back to the seed, brothers. It makes you think.

Clearly they do not like us. They've gone away,
Given up. And who could blame
Anything else for doing the same?
I notice that certain trees look smaller today.

You can't escape the fact: there's a backward trend
From oak to acorn, and from pine
To cone; they all want to resign.
Understandable enough, but where does it end?

Harder, you'd think, for animals; yet the cat
Was pregnant, but has not produced.
Her rounded belly is reduced,
Somehow, to normal. How to answer that?

Buildings, perhaps, will be the next to go;
Imagine it: a tinkle of glass,
A crunch of brick, and a house will pass
Through the soil to the protest meeting below.

This whole conspiracy of inverted birth
Leaves only us; and how shall we
Endure as we deserve to be,
Foolish and lost on the naked skin of the earth?

I RIDE ON MY HIGH BICYCLE

I ride on my high bicycle
Into a sooty Victorian city
Of colonnaded bank buildings,
Horse-troughs, and green marble fountains.

I glide along, contemplating
The curly lettering on the shop-fronts.
An ebony elephant, ten feet tall,
Is wheeled past, advertising something.

When I reach the dark archway
I chain my bicycle to a railing,
Nod to a policeman, climb the steps,
And emerge into unexpected sunshine.

There below lies Caroline Bay,
Its red roofs and its dazzling water.
Now I am running along the path;
It is four o'clock, there is still just time.

I halt and sit on the sandy grass
To remove my shoes and thick stockings;
But something has caught me; around my shoulders
I feel barbed wire; I am entangled.

It pulls my hair, dragging me downwards;
I am suddenly older than seventeen,
Tired, powerless, pessimistic.
I struggle weakly; and wake, of course.

Well, all right. It doesn't matter.
Perhaps I didn't get to the beach:
But I have been there – to all the beaches
(Waking or dreaming) and all the cities.

Now it is very early morning
And from my window I see a leopard
Tall as a horse, majestic and kindly,
Padding over the fallen snow.

PARTING IS SUCH SWEET SORROW

The room is full of clichés – 'Throw me a crumb'
And 'Now I see the writing on the wall'
And 'Don't take umbrage, dear.' I wish I could.
Instead I stand bedazzled by them all,

Longing for shade. Belshazzar's fiery script
Glows there, between the prints of tropical birds,
In neon lighting, and the air is full
Of crumbs that flash and click about me. Words

Glitter in colours like those gaudy prints:
The speech of a computer, metal-based
But feathered like a cloud of darts. All right.
Your signal-system need not go to waste.

Mint me another batch of tokens: say
'I am in your hands; I throw myself upon
Your mercy, casting caution to the winds.'
Thank you; there is no need to go on.

Thus authorized by your mechanical
Issue, I lift you like a bale of hay,
Open the window wide, and toss you out;
And gales of laughter whirl you far away.

HAUNTINGS

Three times I have slept in your house
And this is definitely the last.
I cannot endure the transformations:
Nothing stays the same for an hour.

Last time there was a spiral staircase
Winding across the high room.
People tramped up and down it all night,
Carrying brief-cases, pails of milk, bombs,

Pretending not to notice me
As I lay in a bed lousy with dreams.
Couldn't you have kept them away?
After all, they were trespassing.

14

The time before it was all bathrooms,
Full of naked, quarrelling girls –
And you claim to like solitude:
I do not understand your arrangements.

Now the glass doors to the garden
Open on rows of stone columns;
Beside them stands a golden jeep.
Where are we this time? On what planet?

Every night lasts for a week.
I toss and turn and wander about,
Whirring from room to room like a moth,
Ignored by those indifferent faces.

At last I think I have woken up.
I lift my head from the pillow, rejoicing.
The alarm-clock is playing Schubert:
I am still asleep. This is too much.

Well, I shall try again in a minute.
I shall wake into this real room
With its shadowy plants and patterned screens
(Yes, I remember how it looks).

It will be cool, but I shan't wait
To light the gas-fire. I shall dress
(I know where my clothes are) and slip out.
You needn't think I am here to stay.

ADVICE TO A DISCARDED LOVER

Think, now: if you have found a dead bird,
Not only dead, not only fallen,
But full of maggots: what do you feel –
More pity or more revulsion?

Pity is for the moment of death,
And the moments after. It changes
When decay comes, with the creeping stench
And the wriggling, munching scavengers.

15

Returning later, though, you will see
A shape of clean bone, a few feathers,
An inoffensive symbol of what
Once lived. Nothing to make you shudder.

It is clear then. But perhaps you find
The analogy I have chosen
For our dead affair rather gruesome –
Too unpleasant a comparison.

It is not accidental. In you
I see maggots close to the surface.
You are eaten up by self-pity,
Crawling with unlovable pathos.

If I were to touch you I should feel
Against my fingers fat, moist worm-skin.
Do not ask me for charity now:
Go away until your bones are clean.

THE WATER BELOW

This house is floored with water,
Wall to wall, a deep green pit,
Still and gleaming, edged with stone.
Over it are built stairways
And railed living-areas
In wrought iron. All rather
Impractical; it will be
Damp in winter, and we shall
Surely drop small objects – keys,
Teaspoons, or coins – through the chinks
In the ironwork, to splash
Lost into the glimmering
Depths (and do we know how deep?).
It will have to be rebuilt:
A solid floor of concrete
Over this dark well (perhaps
Already full of coins, like
The flooded crypt of that church
In Ravenna). You might say
It could be drained, made into
A useful cellar for coal.

But I am sure the water
Would return; would never go.
Under my grandmother's house
In Drury, when I was three,
I always believed there was
Water: lift up the floorboards
And you would see it – a lake,
A subterranean sea.
True, I played under the house
And saw only hard-packed earth,
Wooden piles, gardening tools,
A place to hunt for lizards.
That was different: below
I saw no water. Above,
I knew it must still be there,
Waiting. (For why did we say
'Forgive us our trespasses,
Deliver us from evil'?)
Always beneath the safe house
Lies the pool, the hidden sea
Created before we were.
It is not easy to drain
The waters under the earth.

THINK BEFORE YOU SHOOT

Look, children, the wood is full of tigers,
Scorching the bluebells with their breath.
You reach for guns. Will you preserve the flowers
At such cost? Will you prefer the death
Of prowling stripes to a mush of trampled stalks?
Through the eyes, then – do not spoil the head.
Tigers are easier to shoot than to like.
Sweet necrophiles, you only love them dead.

There now, you've got three – and with such fur, too,
Golden and warm and salty. Very good.
Don't expect them to forgive you, though.
There are plenty more of them. This is their wood
(And their bluebells, which you have now forgotten).
They've eaten all the squirrels. They want you,
And it's no excuse to say you're only children.
No one is on your side. What will you do?

17

THE PANGOLIN

There have been all those tigers, of course,
And a leopard, and a six-legged giraffe,
And a young deer that ran up to my window
Before it was killed, and once a blue horse,
And somewhere an impression of massive dogs.
Why do I dream of such large, hot-blooded beasts
Covered with sweating fur and full of passions
When there could be dry lizards and cool frogs,
Or slow, modest creatures, as a rest
From all those panting, people-sized animals?
Hedgehogs or perhaps tortoises would do,
But I think the pangolin would suit me best:
A vegetable animal, who goes
Disguised as an artichoke or asparagus-tip
In a green coat of close-fitting leaves,
With his flat shovel-tail and his pencil-nose:
The scaly anteater. Yes, he would fit
More aptly into a dream than into his cage
In the Small Mammal House; so I invite him
To be dreamt about, if he would care for it.

HIGH TIDE IN THE GARDEN

A GAME

They are throwing the ball
to and fro between them,
in and out of the picture.
She is in the painting
hung on the wall
in a narrow gold frame.
He stands on the floor
catching and tossing ,
at the right distance.
She wears a white dress,
black boots and stockings,
and a flowered straw hat.
She moves in silence
but it seems from her face
that she must be laughing.
Behind her is sunlight
and a tree-filled garden;
you might think to hear
birds or running water,
but no, there is nothing.
Once or twice he has spoken
but does so no more,
for she cannot answer.
So he stands smiling,
playing her game
(she is almost a child),
not daring to go,
intent on the ball.
And she is the same.
For what would result
neither wishes to know
if it should fall.

BOGYMAN

Stepping down from the blackberry bushes
he stands in my path: Bogyman.
He is not as I had remembered him,
though he still wears the broad-brimmed hat,
the rubber-soled shoes and the woollen gloves.
No face; and that soft mooning voice
still spinning its endless distracting yarn.

But this is daylight, a misty autumn
Sunday, not unpopulated
by birds. I can see him in such colours
as he wears – fawn, grey, murky blue –
not all shadow-clothed, as he was that night
when I was ten; he seems less tall
(I have grown) and less muffled in silence.

I have no doubt at all, though, that he is
Bogyman. He is why children
do not sleep all night in their tree-houses.
He is why, when I had pleaded
to spend a night on the common, under
a cosy bush, and my mother'
surprisingly said yes, she took no risk.

He was the risk I would not take; better
to make excuses, to lose face,
than to meet the really faceless, the one
whose name was too childish for us
to utter – 'murderers' we talked of, and
'lunatics escaped from Earlswood'.
But I met him, of course, as we all do.

Well, that was then; I survived; and later
survived meetings with his other
forms, bold or pathetic or disguised – the
slummocking figure in a dark
alley, or the lover turned suddenly
icy-faced; fingers at my throat
and ludicrous violence in kitchens.

I am older now, and (I tell myself,
circling carefully around him
at the far edge of the path, pretending
I am not in fact confronted)
can deal with such things. But what, Bogyman,
shall I be at twice my age? (At
your age?) Shall I be grandmotherly, fond

suddenly of gardening, chatty with
neighbours? Or strained, not giving in,
writing for *Ambit* and hitch-hiking to
Turkey? Or sipping Guinness in
the Bald-Faced Stag, in wrinkled stockings? Or
(and now I look for the first time
straight at you) something like you, Bogyman?

CLARENDON WHATMOUGH

Clarendon Whatmough sits in his chair
telling me that I am hollow.
The walls of his study are dark and bare;
he has his back to the window.
Are you priest or psychiatrist, Clarendon Whatmough?
I do not have to believe you.

The priest in the pub kept patting my hand
more times than I thought needful.
I let him think me a Catholic, and
giggled, and felt quite sinful.
You were not present, Clarendon Whatmough:
I couldn't have flirted with you.

Christopher is no longer a saint
but I still carry the medal
with his image on, which my mother sent
to protect me when I travel.
It pleases her – and me: two
unbelievers, Clarendon Whatmough.

But when a friend was likely to die
I wanted to pray, if I could
after so many years, and feeling shy
of churches walked in the wood.

21

A hypocritical thing to do,
would you say, Clarendon Whatmough?

Or a means of dispelling buried guilt,
a conventional way to ease
my fears? I tell you this: I felt
the sky over the trees
crack open like a nutshell. You
don't believe me, Clarendon Whatmough:

or rather, you would explain that I
induced some kind of reaction
to justify the reversal of my
usual lack of conviction.
No comment from Clarendon Whatmough.
He tells me to continue.

Why lay such critical emphasis
on this other-worldly theme?
I could tell you my sexual fantasies
as revealed in my latest dream.
Do, if you wish, says Clarendon Whatmough:
it's what I expect of you.

Clarendon Whatmough doesn't sneer;
he favours a calm expression,
prefers to look lofty and austere
and let me display an emotion
then anatomize it. Clarendon Whatmough,
shall I analyse you?

No: that would afford me even less
amusement than I provide.
We may both very well be centreless,
but I will not look inside
your shadowy eyes; nor shall you
now, in my open ones, Clarendon Whatmough.

I leave you fixed in your formal chair,
your ambiguous face unseeing,
and go, thankful that I'm aware
at least of my own being.
Who is convinced, though, Clarendon Whatmough,
of your existence? Are you?

A SURPRISE IN THE PENINSULA

When I came in that night I found
the skin of a dog stretched flat and
nailed upon my wall between the
two windows. It seemed freshly killed –
there was blood at the edges. Not
my dog: I have never owned one,
I rather dislike them. (Perhaps
whoever did it knew that.) It
was a light brown dog, with smooth hair;
no head, but the tail still remained.
On the flat surface of the pelt
was branded the outline of the
peninsula, singed in thick black
strokes into the fur: a coarse map.
The position of the town was
marked by a bullet-hole; it went
right through the wall. I placed my eye
to it, and could see the dark trees
outside the house, flecked with moonlight.
I locked the door then, and sat up
all night, drinking small cups of the
bitter local coffee. A dog
would have been useful, I thought, for
protection. But perhaps the one
I had been given performed that
function; for no one came that night,
nor for three more. On the fourth day
it was time to leave. The dog-skin
still hung on the wall, stiff and dry
by now, the flies and the smell gone.
Could it, I wondered, have been meant
not as a warning, but a gift?
And, scarcely shuddering, I drew
the nails out and took it with me.

PURPLE SHINING LILIES

The events of the Aeneid were not enacted
on a porridge-coloured plain; although my
greyish pencilled-over Oxford text
is monochrome, tends to deny
the flaming pyre, that fearful tawny light,
the daily colour-productions in the sky

(dawn variously rosy); Charon's boat
mussel-shell blue on the reedy mud
of Styx; the wolf-twins in a green cave;
huge Triton rising from the flood
to trumpet on his sky-coloured conch;
and everywhere the gleam of gold and blood.

Cybele's priest rode glittering into battle
on a bronze-armoured horse: his great bow
of gold, his cloak saffron, he himself
splendid in *ferrugine et ostro* –
rust and shellfish. (We laugh, but Camilla
for this red and purple gear saw fit to go

to her death.) The names, indeed, are as foreign
in their resonances as the battle-rite:
luteus with its vaguely medical air;
grim *ater*; or the two versions of white:
albus thick and eggy; *candidus*
clear as a candle-flame's transparent light.

It dazzled me, that white, when I was young;
that and *purpureus* – poppy-red,
scarlet, we were firmly taught, not purple
in the given context; but inside my head
the word was both something more than visual
and also exactly what it said.

Poppies and lilies mixed (the mystical
and the moral?) was what I came upon.
My eyes leaping across the juxtaposed
adjectives, I saw them both as one,
and brooded secretly upon the image:
purple shining lilies, bright in the sun.

AFTERWARDS

We weave haunted circles about each other,
advance and retreat in turn, like witchdoctors
before a fetish. Yes, you are right to fear
me now, and I you. But love, this ritual
will exhaust us. Come closer. Listen. Be brave.
I am going to talk to you quietly
as sometimes, in the long past (you remember?),
we made love. Let us be intent, and still. Still.
There are ways of approaching it. This is one:
this gentle talk, with no pause for suspicion,
no hesitation, because you do not know
the thing is upon you, until it has come –
now, and you did not even hear it.
                                        Silence
is what I am trying to achieve for us.
A nothingness, a non-relatedness, this
unknowing into which we are sliding now
together: this will have to be our kingdom.

Rain is falling. Listen to the gentle rain.

HAPPY ENDING

After they had not made love
she pulled the sheet up over her eyes
until he was buttoning his shirt:
not shyness for their bodies – those
they had willingly displayed – but a frail
endeavour to apologise.

Later, though, drawn together by
a distaste for such 'untidy ends'
they agreed to meet again; whereupon
they giggled, reminisced, held hands
as though what they had made was love –
and not that happier outcome, friends.

BEING BLIND

(For Meg Sheffield)

Listen to that:
it is the sea rushing across the garden
swamping the apple tree, beating against the house,
carrying white petals; the sea from France
coming to us.
                    It is the April wind
I tell myself, but cannot rise to look.

You were talking about your blind friend –
how you had to share a room with her once
on holiday, and in the night you woke:
she was staring at you. Was she really blind?
You leaned over her bed for a long time,
watching her, trying to understand,
suppressing unworthy, unendurable
speculations (if she could see
what kind of creature was she?) until
her eyes went swivelling in a dream
as ours do, closed. Yes: blind.

Then I came to bed and, thinking of her
for whom eyelids have no particular purpose,
closed mine. And now there is this sound
of a savage tide rushing towards me.
Do you, in the front of the house, hear it?
I cannot look out. I am blind now.
If I walk downstairs, hand on the banister
(as she did once – admiring, she told us,
our Christmas lights), if I open the door
it will swish and swill over my feet:
the sea. Listen.

GRANDMA

It was the midnight train; I was tired and edgy.
The advertisement portrayed – I wrote it down – a
'Skull-like young female, licking lips' and I added
'Prefer Grandma, even dead' as she newly was.
I walked home singing one of her Irish ballads.

Death is one thing, necrophilia another.

So I climbed up that ladder in the frescoed barn –
a soft ladder, swaying and collapsing under
my feet (my hands alone hauled me into the loft) –
and found, without surprise, a decomposed lady
who drew me down to her breast, with her disengaged
armbones, saying 'Come, my dearie, don't be afraid,
come to me' into a mess of sweetish decay.

It was a dream. I screamed and woke, put on the light,
dozed, woke again. For half a day I carried that
carcass in my own failing arms. Then remembered:
even the dead want to be loved for their own sake.
She was indeed my grandmother. She did not choose
to be dead and rotten. My blood too (Group A,
Rhesus negative, derived exactly from hers)
will suffer that deterioration; my much
modified version of her nose will fall away,
my longer bones collapse like hers. So let me now
apologise to my sons and their possible
children for the gruesomeness: we do not mean it.

NGAURANGA GORGE HILL

The bee in the foxglove, the mouth on the nipple,
the hand between the thighs.
                            Forgive me
these procreative images.
                        Do you remember
that great hill outside Wellington, which we

had to climb, before they built the motorway,
to go north? The engine used to boil
in the old Chev. Straight up the road went
and tipped us over into Johnsonville.

Nothing on the way but rock and gorse, gravel-
pits, and foxgloves; and a tunnel hacked deep,
somewhere, into a cliff. Ah, my burgeoning new
country, I said (being fourteen). Yes, a steep

road to climb. But coming back was better;
a matter for some caution in a car,
but glorious and terrible on a bicycle.
Heart in my pedals, down I would roar

towards the sea; I'd go straight into it
if I didn't brake. No time then to stare
self-consciously at New Zealand vegetation,
at the awkward landscape. I needed all my care

for making the right turn towards the city
at the hill's base, where the paint-hoarding stood
between me and the harbour.
                               For ten years
that city possessed me. In time it bred

two sons for me (little pink mouths tucked
like foxglove-bells over my nipples). Yes,
in this matter Wellington and I have no
quarrel. But I think it was a barren place.

STEWART ISLAND

'But look at all this beauty'
said the hotel manager's wife
when asked how she could bear to
live there. True: there was a fine bay,
all hills and atmosphere; white
sand, and bush down to the sea's edge;
oyster-boats, too, and Maori
fishermen with Scottish names (she
ran off with one that autumn).
As for me, I walked on the beach;
it was too cold to swim. My
seven-year-old collected shells
and was bitten by sandflies;
my four-year-old paddled, until
a mad seagull jetted down
to jab its claws and beak into
his head. I had already
decided to leave the country.

ON A SON RETURNED TO NEW ZEALAND

He is my green branch growing in a far plantation.
He is my first invention.

No one can be in two places at once.
So we left Athens on the same morning.
I was in a hot railway carriage, crammed
between Serbian soldiers and peasant
women, on sticky seats, with nothing to
drink but warm mineral water.
                                                    He was
in a cabin with square windows, sailing
across the Mediterranean, fast,
to Suez.
            Then I was back in London
in the tarnished summer, remembering,
as I folded his bed up, and sent the
television set away. Letters came
from Aden and Singapore, late.
                                                    He was
already in his father's house, on the
cliff-top, where the winter storms roll across
from Kapiti Island, and the flax bends
before the wind. He could go no further.

He is my bright sea-bird on a rocky beach.

SATURDAY

I am sitting on the step
drinking coffee and
smoking, listening to jazz.
The smoke separates
two scents: fresh paint in the house
behind me; in front,
buddleia.
            The neighbours cut
back our lilac tree –
it shaded their neat garden.
The buddleia will
be next, no doubt; but bees and

all those butterflies
approve of our shaggy trees.

*

I am painting the front door
with such thick juicy
paint I could almost eat it.
People going past
with their shopping stare at my
bare legs and old shirt.
The door will be sea-green.
                          Our
black cat walked across
the painted step and left a
delicate paw-trail.
I swore at her and frightened
two little girls – this
street is given to children.

The other cat is younger,
white and tabby, fat,
with a hoarse voice. In summer
she sleeps all day long
in the rosebay willow-herb,
too lazy to walk
on paint.
            Andrew is upstairs;
having discovered
quick-drying non-drip gloss, he
is old enough now
to paint all his furniture
tangerine and the
woodwork green; he is singing.

*

I am lying in the sun,
in the garden. Bees
dive on white clover beside
my ears. The sky is
Greek blue, with a vapour-trail
chalked right across it.
My transistor radio
talks about the moon.

*

I am floating in the sky.
Below me the house
crouches among its trees like
a cat in long grass.
I want to stroke its roof-ridge
but I think I can
already hear it purring.

TREES

Elm, laburnum, hawthorn, oak:
all the incredible leaves expand
on their dusty branches, like
Japanese paper flowers in water,
like anything one hardly believes
will really work this time; and
I am a stupefied spectator
as usual. What are they all, these
multiverdant, variously-made
soft sudden things, these leaves?
So I walk solemnly in the park
with a copy of *Let's Look at Trees*
from the children's library,
identifying leaf-shapes and bark
while behind my back, at home,
my own garden is turning into a wood.
Before my house the pink may tree
lolls its heavy heads over mine
to grapple my hair as I come
in; at the back door I walk out
under lilac. The two elders
(I let them grow for the wine)
hang vastly over the fence, no doubt
infuriating my tidy neighbours.
In the centre the apple tree
needs pruning. And everywhere,
soaring over the garden shed,
camouflaged by roses, or snaking
up through the grass like vertical worms,
grows every size of sycamore.
Last year we attacked them; I saw
my son, so tender to ants, so sad

over dead caterpillars, hacking
at living roots as thick as his arms,
drenching the stumps with creosote.
No use: they continue to grow.
Under the grass, the ground
must be peppered with winged seeds,
meshed with a tough stringy net
of roots; and the house itself undermined
by wandering wood. Shall we see
the floorboards lifted one morning
by these indomitable weeds,
or find in the airing-cupboard
a rather pale sapling?
And if we do, will it be
worse than cracked pipes or dry rot?
Trees I can tolerate; they are why
I chose this house – for the apple tree,
elder, buddleia, lilac, may;
and outside my bedroom window, higher
every week, its leaves unfurling
pink at the twig-tips (composite
in form) the tallest sycamore.

COUNTRY STATION

First she made a little garden
of sorrel stalks wedged among
some yellowy-brown moss-cushions

and fenced it with ice-lolly sticks
(there were just enough); then she
set out biscuit-crumbs on a brick

for the ants; now she sits on a
deserted luggage-trolley
to watch them come for their dinner.

It's nice here – cloudy but quite warm.
Five trains have swooshed through, and one
stopped, but at the other platform.

Later, when no one is looking,
she may climb the roof of that
low shed. Her mother is making

another telephone call (she
isn't crying any more).
Perhaps they will stay here all day.

THE THREE-TOED SLOTH

The three-toed sloth is the slowest creature we know
for its size. It spends its life hanging upside-down
from a branch, its baby nestling on its breast.
It never cleans itself, but lets fungus grow
on its fur. The grin it wears, like an idiot clown,
proclaims the joys of a life which is one long rest.

The three-toed sloth is content. It doesn't care.
It moves imperceptibly, like the laziest snail
you ever saw blown up to the size of a sheep.
Disguised as a grey-green bough it dangles there
in the steamy Amazon jungle. That long-drawn wail
is its slow-motion sneeze. Then it falls asleep.

One cannot but envy such torpor. Its top speed,
when rushing to save its young, is a dramatic
fourteen feet per minute, in a race with fate.
The puzzle is this, though: how did nature breed
a race so determinedly unenergetic?
What passion ever inspired a sloth to mate?

AGAINST COUPLING

I write in praise of the solitary act:
of not feeling a trespassing tongue
forced into one's mouth, one's breath
smothered, nipples crushed against the
ribcage, and that metallic tingling
in the chin set off by a certain odd nerve:

unpleasure. Just to avoid those eyes would help –
such eyes as a young girl draws life from,
listening to the vegetal
rustle within her, as his gaze
stirs polypal fronds in the obscure
sea-bed of her body, and her own eyes blur.

There is much to be said for abandoning
this no longer novel exercise –
for not 'participating in
a total experience' – when
one feels like the lady in Leeds who
had seen *The Sound of Music* eighty-six times;

or more, perhaps, like the school drama mistress
producing *A Midsummer Night's Dream*
for the seventh year running, with
yet another cast from 5B.
Pyramus and Thisbe are dead, but
the hole in the wall can still be troublesome.

I advise you, then, to embrace it without
encumbrance. No need to set the scene,
dress up (or undress), make speeches.
Five minutes of solitude are
enough – in the bath, or to fill
that gap between the Sunday papers and lunch.

MORNINGS AFTER

The surface dreams are easily remembered:
I wake most often with a comforting sense
of having seen a pleasantly odd film –
nothing too outlandish or too intense;

of having, perhaps, befriended animals,
made love, swum the Channel, flown in the air
without wings, visited Tibet or Chile:
simple childish stuff. Or else the rare

34

recurrent horror makes its call upon me:
I dream one of my sons is lost or dead,
or that I am trapped in a tunnel underground;
but my scream is enough to recall me to my bed.

Sometimes, indeed, I congratulate myself
on the nice precision of my observation:
on having seen so vividly a certain
colour; having felt the sharp sensation

of cold water on my hands; the exact taste
of wine or peppermints. I take a pride
in finding all my senses operative
even in sleep. So, with nothing to hide,

I amble through my latest entertainment
again, in the bath or going to work,
idly amused at what the night has offered;
unless this is a day when a sick jerk

recalls to me a sudden different vision:
I see myself inspecting the vast slit
of a sagging whore; making love with a hunchbacked
hermaphrodite; eating worms or shit;

or rapt upon necrophily or incest.
And whatever loathsome images I see
are just as vivid as the pleasant others.
I flush and shudder: my God, was that me?

Did I invent so ludicrously revolting
a scene? And if so, how could I forget
until this instant? And why now remember?
Furthermore (and more disturbing yet)

are all my other forgotten dreams like these?
Do I, for hours of my innocent nights,
wallow content and charmed through verminous muck,
rollick in the embraces of such frights?

And are the comic or harmless fantasies
I wake with merely a deceiving guard,
as one might put a Hans Andersen cover
on a volume of the writings of De Sade?

Enough, enough. Bring back those easy pictures,
Tibet or antelopes, a seemly lover,
or even the black tunnel. For the rest,
I do not care to know. Replace the cover.

GAS

1

You recognize a body by its blemishes:
moles and birthmarks, scars, tattoos, oddly formed
    earlobes.
The present examination must be managed
in darkness, and by touch alone. That should suffice.
Starting at the head, then, there is a small hairless
scar on the left eyebrow; the bridge of the nose flat;
crowded lower teeth, and a chipped upper canine
(the lips part to let my fingers explore); a mole
on the right side of the neck.
                    No need to go on:
I know it all. But as I draw away, a hand
grips mine: a hand whose thumb bends back as mine
    does, whose
third finger bears the torn nail I broke in the door
last Thursday; and I feel these fingers check the scar
on my knuckle, measure my wrist's circumference,
move on gently exploring towards my elbow . . .

2

It was gas, we think.
Insects and reptiles survived it
and most of the birds;
also the larger mammals – grown
cattle, a few sheep,
horses, the landlord's Alsatian
(I shall miss the cats)
and, in this village, about a
fifth of the people.
It culled scientifically
within a fixed range,
sparing the insignificant
and the chosen strong.
It let us sleep for fourteen hours

36

and wake, not caring
whether we woke or not, in a
soft antiseptic
silence. There was a faint odour
of furniture-wax.
We know now, of course, more or less
what happened, but then
it was rather puzzling: to wake
from a thick dark sleep
lying on the carpeted floor
in the saloon bar
of the Coach and Horses; to sense
others lying near,
very still; and nearest to me
this new second self.

3
I had one history until today:
now I shall have two.
No matter how nicely she may contrive
to do what I do
there are two hearts now for our identical
blood to pass through.

Nothing can change her. Whether she walks by my side
like a silly twin
or dyes her hair, adopts a new accent,
disguises her skin
with make-up and suntan, she cannot alter
the creature within.

She sees with my imperfect vision, she wears
my finger-prints; she is made
from me. If she should break the bones I gave her,
if disease should invade
her replicas of my limbs and organs,
which of us is betrayed?

4
How was she torn out of me? Was it the
urgent wrench of birth, a matter of hard
breathless shoving (but there is no blood) or

Eve from Adam's rib, quick and surgical
(but there is no scar) or did I burgeon
with fleshy buds along my limbs, growing
a new substance from that gas I drank in,
to double myself? Did I perform the
amoeba's trick of separating into
two loose amorphous halves, a heart in each?
Or was my skin slipped off like the skin of
a peanut, to reveal two neat sections,
face to face and identical, within?
Yes, we had better say it was like this:
for if it was birth, which was the mother?
Since both have equal rights to our past, she
might justly claim to have created me.

5

It is the sixth day
now, and nothing much has happened.
Those of us who are
double (all the living ones) go
about our business.
The two Mrs Hudsons bake bread
in the pub kitchen
and contrive meals from what is left –
few shops are open.
The two Patricks serve in the bar
(Bill Hudson is dead).
I and my new sister stay here –
it seems easiest –
and help with the housework; sometimes
we go for walks, or
play darts or chess, finding ourselves
not as evenly
matched as we might have expected:
our capacity
is equal, but our moods vary.
These things occupy
the nights – none of us need sleep now.
Only the dead sleep
laid out in all the beds upstairs.
They do not decay,
(some effect of the gas) and this
seemed a practical

and not irreverent means of
dealing with them. My
dead friend from London
and a housemaid from the hotel
lie in the bedroom
where we two go to change our clothes.
This evening when we
had done our hair before dinner
we combed and arranged
theirs too.

6

Saturday night in the bar; eight couples
fill it well enough: twin schoolteachers, two
of the young man from the garage, four girls
from the shop next door, some lads from the farms.
These woodenly try to chat up the girls,
but without heart. There is no sex now, when
each has his undeniable partner,
and no eyes or hands for any other.
Division, not union, is the way we
must reproduce now. Nor can one think with
desire or even curiosity
of one's identical other. How lust
for what is utterly familiar?
How place an auto-erotic hand on
a thigh which matches one's own? So we chat
about local events: the twin calves born,
it seems, on every farm; the corpse
in a well, and the water quite unspoiled;
the Post Office reopened, but with no
telephone links to places further than
the next town – just as there are no programmes
on television or radio, and
the single newspaper that we have seen
(a local one) contained only poems.
No one cares much for communication
outside this circle. I am forgetting
my work in London, my old concerns (we
laugh about the unpaid rent, the office
unmanned, the overdue library books).
They did a good job, whoever they were.

7

Two patterns of leaves above me: laurel
rather low, on my right,
and high on my left sycamore; a sky
pale grey: dawn or twilight.

Dew on my face, and on the gravel path
on which I am lying.
That scent of wax in the air, and a few
birds beginning to sing.

My mind is hazed by a long sleep – the first
for days. But I can tell
how it has been: the gas caught us walking
on this path, and we fell.

I feel a crystal, carolling lightness.
Beside me I can see
my newest self. It has happened again:
division, more of me.

Four, perhaps? We two stand up together,
dazed, euphoric, and go
to seek out our matching others, knowing
that they should be two, now.

My partner had been walking, I recall,
a little way ahead.
We find her. But there is only one. I
look upon myself, dead.

8

This is becoming ridiculous:
the gas visits us regularly,
dealing out death or duplication.
I am eight people now – and four dead
(these propped up against the trees in the
gardens, by the gravel walk). We eight
have inherited the pub, and shall,
if we continue to display our
qualities of durability,
inherit the village, God help us.
I see my image everywhere –

feeding the hens, hoeing the spinach,
peeling the potatoes, devising
a clever dish with cabbage and eggs.
I am responsible with and for
all. If B (we go by letters now)
forgets to light the fire, I likewise
have forgotten. If C breaks a cup
we all broke it. I am eight people,
a kind of octopus or spider,
and I cannot say it pleases me.
Sitting through our long sleepless nights, we
no longer play chess or poker (eight
identical hands, in which only
the cards are different). Now, instead,
we plan our death. Not quite suicide,
but a childish game: when the gas comes
(we can predict the time within a
margin of two days) we shall take care
to be in dangerous places. I can
see us all, wading in the river
for hours, taking long baths, finding
ladders and climbing to paint windows
on the third storey. It will be fun –
something, at last, to entertain us.

9
Winter. The village is silent –
no lights in the windows, and
a corpse in every snowdrift.
The electricity failed
months ago. We have chopped down half
the orchard for firewood,
and live on the apples we picked
in autumn. (That was a fine
harvest-day: three of us fell down
from high trees when the gas came.)
One way and another, in fact,
we are reduced now to two –
it can never be one alone,
for the survivor always
wakes with a twin.
                    We have great hopes
of the snow. At this moment

41

she is standing outside in it
like Socrates. We work shifts,
two hours each. But this evening
when gas-time will be closer
we are going to take blankets
and make up beds in the snow –
as if we were still capable
of sleep. And indeed, it may
come to us there: our only sleep.

10

Come, gentle gas

I lie and look at the night.
The stars look normal enough –
it has nothing to do with them –
and no new satellite
or comet has shown itself.
There is nothing up there to blame.

Come from wherever

She is quiet by my side.
I cannot see her breath
in the frost-purified air.
I would say she had died
if so natural a death
were possible now, here.

Come with what death there is

You have killed almost a score
of the bodies you made
from my basic design.
I offer you two more.
Let the mould be destroyed:
it is no longer mine.

Come, then, secret scented double-dealing gas.
We are cold: come and warm us.
We are tired: come and lull us.
Complete us.
Come. Please.

THE SCENIC ROUTE

THE BULLAUN

'Drink water from the hollow in the stone . . . '
This was it, then – the cure for madness:
a rock with two round cavities, filled with rain;
a thing I'd read about once, and needed then,
but since forgotten. I didn't expect it here –
not having read the guidebook;
not having planned, even, to be in Antrim.
'There's a round tower, isn't there?' I'd asked.
The friendly woman in the post office
gave me directions: 'Up there past the station,
keep left, on a way further – it's a fair bit –
and have you been to Lough Neagh yet?' I walked –
it wasn't more than a mile – to the stone phallus
rising above its fuzz of beech-trees
in the municipal gardens. And beside it,
this. I circled around them,
backing away over wet grass and beechmast,
aiming the camera (since I had it with me,
since I was playing tourist this afternoon)
and saw two little boys pelting across.
'Take our photo! Take our photo! Please!'
We talked it over for a bit –
how I couldn't produce one then and there;
but could I send it to them with the postman?
Well, could they give me their addresses?
Kevin Tierney and Declan McCallion,
Tobergill Gardens. I wrote, they stood and smiled,
I clicked, and waved goodbye, and went.
Two miles away, an hour later,
heading dutifully through the damp golf-course
to Lough Neagh, I thought about the rock,
wanting it. Not for my own salvation;
hardly at all for me: for sick Belfast,
for the gunmen and the slogan-writers,
for the poor crazy girl I met in the station,

for Kevin and Declan, who would soon mistrust
all camera-carrying strangers. But of course
the thing's already theirs: a monument,
a functionless, archaic, pitted stone
and a few mouthfuls of black rainwater.

PLEASE IDENTIFY YOURSELF

British, more or less; Anglican, of a kind.
In Cookstown I dodge the less urgent question
when a friendly Ulsterbus driver raises it;
'You're not a Moneymore girl yourself?' he asks,
deadpan. I make a cowardly retrogression,
slip ten years back. 'No, I'm from New Zealand.'
'Are you now? Well, that's a coincidence:
the priest at Moneymore's a New Zealander.'
And there's the second question, unspoken.
Unanswered.
             I go to Moneymore
anonymously, and stare at all three churches.

In Belfast, though, where sides have to be taken,
I stop compromising – not that you'd guess,
seeing me hatless there among the hatted,
neutral voyeur among the shining faces
in the glossy Martyrs' Memorial Free Church.
The man himself is cheerleader in the pulpit
for crusader choruses: we're laved in blood,
marshalled in ranks. I chant the nursery tunes
and mentally cross myself. You can't stir me
with evangelistic hymns, Dr Paisley:
I know them. Nor with your computer-planned
sermon – Babylon, Revelation, whispers
of popery, slams at the IRA, more blood.
I scrawl incredulous notes under my hymnbook
and burn with Catholicism.
                          Later
hacking along the Lower Falls Road
against a gale, in my clerical black coat,
I meet a bright gust of tinselly children
in beads and lipstick and their mothers' dresses
for Hallowe'en; who chatter and surround me.

44

Over-reacting once again (a custom
of the country, not mine alone) I give them
all my loose change for their rattling tin
and my blessing – little enough. But now
to my tough Presbyterian ancestors,
Brooks and Hamilton, lying in the graves
I couldn't find at Moneymore and Cookstown
among so many unlabelled bones, I say:
I embrace you also, my dears.

RICHEY

My great-grandfather Richey Brooks
began in mud: at Moneymore;
'a place of mud and nothing else'
he called it (not the way it looks,
but what lies under those green hills?)
Emigrated in '74;
ended in Drury: mud again –
slipped in the duck-run at ninety-three
(wouldn't give up keeping poultry,
always had to farm something).
Caught pneumonia; died saying
'Do you remember Martha Hamilton
of the Oritor Road?' – still courting
the same girl in his mind. And she
lived after him, fierce widow,
in their daughter's house; watched the plumtree –
the gnarled, sappy branches, the yellow
fruit. Ways of living and dying.

THE VOYAGE OUT

The weekly dietary scale
per adult: pork and Indian beef,
three pounds together; one of sugar,
two of potatoes, three and a half
of flour; a gill of vinegar;
salt, pepper, a pint of oatmeal;
coffee, two ounces, likewise tea;

45

six of butter, suet, treacle,
and, in the tropics, of lime-juice;
grudging grants of mustard and pickle;
split peas, raisins, currants, rice,
and half a pound of biscuit a day.
A diet for the young and fit:
monotonous, but not starvation –
and Martha traded half her ration
for extra lime-juice from the crew.
Their quarters, also, adequate.
So not the middle passage; no.
But not a pleasure-cruise, either.
A hundred days of travelling steerage
under capricious canvas; Martha
newly pregnant, struggling to manage
the first four (Tom, Eliza, Joe,
Annie); to keep them cool and clean
from a two-gallon can of water;
to calm their sleeping; to stay awake,
so heavy, herself; to protect the daughter
she rocked unborn in the swaying hammock
below her ribs (who would be Jane).
True, the family was together.
But who could envy Martha? Sick
with salt meat; thirsty; and gazing on
a sky huge as the whole Atlantic,
storm-waves like Slieve Gallion,
and no more Ireland than went with her.

TRAIN FROM THE HOOK OF HOLLAND

Not pill-boxes, exactly: blocks
of concrete, octagonal, serrated –
house-sized fancy buttons, roofed
with green turf. 'Hitler's Atlantic wall'
says the man in the corner seat.
On the other side of the train
lambs running, and, yes, a canal.
Then the low sun through a sea-haze
neon-red over – Maassluis, is it?

46

Some things, once you've got them,
are difficult to get rid of.
But we are happy, going somewhere.

NELIA

She writes to me from a stony island
where they understand none of her languages.
Time has slipped out of its cogwheel:
she walks looking at plants and insects,
thinking without words, forgetting her home
and her work and her callous, temporary young lover.
Her children play like cicadas among the hills
and are safe. She cooks when they are hungry,
sleeps at will, wakes and runs to the sea.
I remember exactly the colour of her daughter's eyes –
glass-green; and the boy's light blue against his tan;
hers less clearly. But I see them now
as blue-black, reflecting an inky sky –
pure, without motes or atmosphere – that extends
uninterrupted from her to the still sun.

MOA POINT

At Moa Point that afternoon
two biologists were searching rockpools
for specimens. It was low tide.
I watched. They rolled away a stone,
fossicked in wet weed, described things
rather self-consciously to each other.
Then one of them put into my hands
a cold heavy jelly: my first sea-slug.
I peered gratefully down at it,
turned it over – did nothing, surely?
for them to laugh at. 'See that?'
said the one with freckles (they were both quite young)
'it doesn't seem to worry her.'
'Oh, well,' said the other 'these local kids . . . '
I kept my eyes down for a moment
in solemn, scientific study;

47

then said in my recently-acquired
almost local accent 'Thank you.'
And firmly but gently (a vet with a kitten)
handed it back.

BRIDDES

'Briddes' he used to call them,
out of Chaucer – those cool
early-morning creatures
who tinkled in the elm-trees.
Briddes talked us awake
and punctuated our childish
medieval loving.
All other birds were birds.

THE FAMOUS TRAITOR

His jailer trod on a rose-petal.
There were others on the stone floor.
His desk tidy; some lines in pencil,
the bible open.
                    Years before
he'd lived like a private soldier –
a bag of nuts and the milk ration
for long days' marches. And under
the uniform a mathematician.
Puzzle-maker. After power:
which he got, this pastor's son
turned agnostic.
                    The nature
of his 'new kind of treason',
his links with the Nazi high command,
the deals, the sense of mission,
are well-documented; and
beyond every explanation.

He died 'with dignity' some said;
some that he had to wait an hour,
died shivering in the bitter cold.

It looked like fear. It was fear:
or it was not. And he did,
or did not, shake hands before
that moment with the firing-squad.
Authorities let us down here.
His final audience, the 'crowd
of notables', might as well
have been, as he was, blindfold.
We are left with the empty cell
like a film-set; the table
where the man of action/dreamer
made notes on his father's bible
in a litter of roses. Enter
his faithful jailer, to record
just this. The rest remains obscure
like all that made a dictionary word
of his name; like what he did it for.

SCRIPT

'Wet the tea, Jinny, the men are back:
I can hear them out there, talking, with the horses',
my mother's grandmother said. They both heard it,
she and her daughter – the wagon bumpily halted,
a rattle of harness, two familiar voices
in sentences to be identified later
and quoted endlessly. But the tea was cold
when the men came in. They'd been six miles away,
pausing to rest on Manurewa Hill
in a grove of trees – whence 'Fetch the nosebags, Dickie'
came clearly over. A freak wind, maybe:
soundwaves carrying, their words lifted up
and dropped on Drury. Eighty years ago,
long before the wireless was invented,
Grandma told us. It made a good story:
baffling. But then, so was the real thing –
radio.
        My father understood it.
Out on the bush farm at Te Rau a Moa
as a teenager he patiently constructed
little fiddly devices, sat for hours
every day adjusting a cat's whisker,

filtering morse through headphones. Later came
loudspeakers, and the whole family could gather
to hear the creaky music of 1YA.
So my father's people were technicians, is that it?
And my mother's were communicators, yes? –
Who worked as a barber in the evenings
for the talking's sake? Who became a teacher –
and who was in love with tractors? No prizes.
Don't classify. Leave the air-waves open.

We each extract what we most need. My sons
rig out their rooms with stereo equipment.
I walk dozily through the house
in the mornings with a neat black box,
audible newspaper, timekeeper and -saver,
sufficient for days like that.
                                    On days like this
I sit in my own high borrowed grove
and let the leafy air clear my mind
for reception. The slow pigeon-flight,
the scraped-wire pipping of some bird,
the loamy scent, offer themselves to me
as little presents, part of an exchange
to be continued and continually
(is this a rondo? that professor asked)
perpetuated. It is not like music,
though the effects can strike as music does:
it is more like agriculture, a nourishing
of the growth-mechanisms, a taking-in
of food for what will flower and seed and sprout.

On a path in the wood two white-haired women
are marching arm in arm, singing a hymn.
A girl stops me to ask where I bought my sandals.
I say 'In Italy, I think' and we laugh.
I am astonished several times a day.
When I get home I shall make tea or coffee
for whoever is there, talk and listen to talk,
share food and living-space. There will always
be time to reassemble the frail components
of this afternoon, to winnow the scattered sounds
dropped into my range, and rescue from them
a seed-hoard for transmission. There will be
always the taking-in and the sending-out.

50

IN MEMORIAM: JAMES K. BAXTER

Dear Jim, I'm using a Shakespearian form
to write you what I'll call a farewell letter.
Rhyming iambics have become the norm
for verse epistles, and I'm no trendsetter.
Perhaps you'll think it's going back a bit,
but as a craftsman you'll approve of it.

What better model have we, after all?
Dylan the Welshman, long your youthful passion,
doesn't quite do now, and the dying fall
of Eliot was never in your fashion.
Of North Americans the one you'd favour
is Lowell. But his salt has the wrong savour:

our ocean's called Pacific, not Atlantic –
which doesn't mean to say Neruda meets
the case. As for the classically romantic –
well, maybe it was easier for Keats:
I'd write with more conviction about death
if it were clutching at my every breath.

And now we've come to it. The subject's out:
the ineluctable, the all-pervasive.
Your death is what this letter's all about;
and if so far I've seemed a bit evasive
it's not from cowardice or phoney tact –
it's simply that I can't believe the fact.

I'd put you, with New Zealand, in cold storage
to wait for my return (should I so choose).
News of destruction can't delete an image:
what isn't seen to go, one doesn't lose.
The bulldozed streets, the buildings they've torn down
remain untouched until I'm back in town.

And so with you, framed in that sepia vision
a hemisphere away from me, and half
the twenty years I've known you. Such division
converts a face into a photograph:
a little blurred perhaps, the outlines dim,
but fixed, enduring, permanently Jim.

I saw you first when I was seventeen,
a word-struck student, ripe for dazzling. You
held unassuming court in the canteen —
the famous poet in the coffee-queue.
I watched with awe. But soon, as spheres are apt
to do in Wellington, ours overlapped.

I married, you might say, into the art.
You were my husband's friend; you'd wander in
on your way home from teaching, at the start,
for literary shop-talk over gin.
And then those fabled parties of one's youth:
home-brew and hot-lines to poetic truth.

Later the drinks were tea and lemonade,
the visits family ones, the talk less vatic;
and later still, down south, after I'd made
my getaway, came idiosyncratic
letters, your generous comments on my verse,
and poems of your own. But why rehearse

matters which you, acute observer, wise
recorder, don't forget? And now I falter,
knowing your present case: those tolerant eyes
will register no more. But I can't alter
this message to a dirge; the public attitude
isn't my style: I write in simple gratitude.

To think of elegies is to recall
several of yours. I find, when I look through
your varied, eloquent poems, nearly all
frosted with hints at death. What can I do
now, when it has become your own condition,
but praise all that you gave to the tradition?

ST JOHN'S SCHOOL

When I went back the school was rather small
but not unexpectedly or oddly so.
I peered in at the windows of the hall
where we sang O God Our Help thirty years ago
for D-Day, the Normandy landings. It was all
as I'd pictured it. Outside, they'd cut the row

of dusty laurels, laid a lawn instead,
and the prefab classroom at the end was new;
but there were the lavatories, there was the shed
where we sat on rainy days with nothing to do,
giggling; and the beech-trees overhead
whose fallen husks we used to riffle through

for triangular nuts. Yes, all as it should be –
no false images to negotiate,
no shocks. I wandered off contentedly
across the playground, out through the north gate,
down the still knee-straining slope, to see
what sprang up suddenly across the street:

the church, that had hardly existed in my past,
that had lurked behind a tree or two, unknown –
and uncensorious of me as I chased
squirrels over the graves – the church had grown:
high on its huge mound it soared, vast;
and God glared out from behind a tombstone.

PUPATION

Books, music, the garden, cats:
I have cocooned myself
in solitude, fatly silken.
Settled?
          I flatter myself.
Things buzz under my ribs;
there are ticklings, dim blunderings.
Ichneumon flies have got in.

THE DROUGHT BREAKS

That wet gravelly sound is rain.
Soil that was bumpy and crumbled
flattens under it, somewhere;
splatters into mud. Spiked grass
grows soft with it and bends like hair.
You lean over me, smiling at last.

KILPECK

We are dried and brittle this morning,
fragile with continence, quiet.
You have brought me to see a church.
I stare at a Norman arch in red sandstone
carved like a Mayan temple-gate;
at serpents writhing up the doorposts
and squat saints with South-American features
who stare back over our heads
from a panel of beasts and fishes.
The gargoyles jutting from under the eaves
are the colour of newborn children.

Last night you asked me
if poetry was the most important thing.

We walk on around the building
craning our heads back to look up
at lions, griffins, fat-faced bears.
The Victorians broke some of these figures
as being too obscene for a church;
but they missed the Whore of Kilpeck.
She leans out under the roof
holding her pink stony cleft agape
with her ancient little hands.
There was always witchcraft here, you say.

The sheep-track up to the fragments
of castle-wall is fringed with bright bushes.
We clamber awkwardly, separate.
Hawthorn and dog-rose offer hips and haws,
orange and crimson capsules, pretending
harvest. I taste a blackberry.
The soil here is coloured like brick-dust,
like the warm sandstone. A fruitful county.
We regard it uneasily.

There is little left to say
after all the talk we had last night
instead of going to bed –
fearful for our originality,
avoiding the sweet obvious act
as if it were the only kind of indulgence.

Silly perhaps.
                    We have our reward.
We are languorous now, heavy
with whatever we were conserving,
carrying each a delicate burden
of choices made or about to be made.
Words whisper hopefully in our heads.

Slithering down the track we hold hands
to keep a necessary balance.
The gargoyles extend their feral faces,
rosy, less lined than ours.
We are wearing out our identities.

FEVERISH

Only a slight fever:
I was not quite out of my mind;
enough to forget my name
and the number and sex of my children
(while clinging to their existence –
three daughters, could it be?)
but not to forget my language
with *Words for Music Perhaps,*
Crazy Jane and the bishop,
galloping through my head.
As for my body, not
quite out of that either:
curled in an S-bend somewhere,
conscious of knees and skull
pressing against a wall
(if I was on my side)
or against a heavy lid
(if I was on my back);
or I could have been face downward
kneeling crouched on a raft,
castaway animal, drifting;
or shrivelled over a desk
head down asleep on it
like Harold, our wasted Orion,
who slept on the bare sand
all those nights in the desert

lightly, head on his briefcase;
who carried the new Peace
to chief after chief, winning
their difficult signatures
by wit and a cool head
under fire and public school charm;
who has now forgotten his Arabic
and the names of his brother's children
and what he did last week;
dozes over an ashtray
or shuffles through *Who was Who*.
Crazy Jane I can take –
the withered breasts that she flaunted,
her fierce remembering tongue;
but spare me his forgetting.
Age is a sad fever.

FOLIE A DEUX

They call it pica,
this ranging after alien tastes:
acorns (a good fresh country food,
better than I'd remembered)
that morning in the wood,

and moonlit roses –
perfumed lettuce, rather unpleasant:
we rinsed them from our teeth with wine.
It seems a shared perversion,
not just a kink of mine –

you were the one
who nibbled the chrysanthemums.
All right: we are avoiding something.
Tonight you are here early.
We seem to lack nothing.

We are alone,
quiet, unhurried. The whisky has
a smoky tang, like dark chocolate.
You speak of ceremony, of
something to celebrate.

I hear the church bells
and suddenly fear blasphemy,
even name it. The word's unusual
between us. But you don't laugh.
We postpone our ritual

and act another:
sit face to face across a table,
talk about places we have known
and friends who are still alive
and poems (not our own).

It works. We are altered
from that fey couple who talked out
fountains of images, a spray
of loves, deaths, dramas, jokes:
their histories; who lay

manic with words,
fingers twined in each other's hair
(no closer) wasting nights and hours;
who chewed, as dry placebos,
those bitter seeds and flowers.

It is the moment.
We rise, and touch at last. And now
without pretence or argument,
fasting, and in our right minds,
go to our sacrament.

ACRIS HIEMS

A letter from that pale city
I escaped from ten years ago
and no good news.
I carry it with me
devising comfortable answers
(the sickness, shall I say?
is not peculiarly yours),
as I walk along Beech Drive,
Church Vale, Ringwood Avenue
at eleven on a Tuesday morning

going nowhere.
A bony day, an invisible wind,
the sky white as an ambulance,
and no one in sight.
Friend, I will say in my letter –
since you call me a friend still,
whatever I have been – forgive me.
Rounding the next corner
I see a van that crawls along
beside the birch-trunks and pink pavements.
A handbell rings from the driver's window:
he has paraffin for sale
and ought to do good business
now that we have power-cuts.
But the painted doors do not open.
The wind in the ornamental hedges
rustles. Nobody comes.
The bell rings. The houses listen.
Bring out your dead.

DECEMBER MORNING

I raise the blind and sit by the window
dry-mouthed, waiting for light.
One needs a modest goal,
something safely attainable.
An hour before sunrise
(due at seven fifty-three)
I go out into the cold new morning
for a proper view of that performance;
walk greedily towards the heath
gulping the blanched air
and come in good time to Kenwood.
They have just opened the gates.
There is a kind of world here, too:
on the grassy slopes above the lake
in the white early Sunday
I see with something like affection
people I do not know
walking their unlovable dogs.

SHOWCASE

Looking through the glass showcase
right into the glass of the shelf,
your eye level with it, not
swerving above it or below,
you see neither the reflected image
nor the object itself.

There is only a swimming horizon,
a watery prison for the sight,
acres of shadowy green jelly,
and no way yet to know
what they support, what stands
in the carefully-angled light.

You take a breath, raise your head,
and see whether the case reveals
Dutch goblet, carved reliquary,
the pope's elaborately-petalled rose
of gold-leaf; or the bronze Cretan
balanced on his neat heels,

and you look, drowning or perhaps
rescued from drowning; and your eyes close.

OVER THE EDGE

All my dead people
seeping through the riverbank where they are buried
colouring the stream pale brown
are why I swim in the river,
feeling now rather closer to them
than when the water was clear,
when I could walk barefoot on the gravel
seeing only the flicker of minnows
possessing nothing but balance.

THE NET

She keeps the memory-game
as a charm against falling in love
and each night she climbs out of the same window
into the same garden with the arch for roses –
no roses, though; and the white snake dead too;
nothing but evergreen shrubs, and grass, and water,
and the wire trellis that will trap her in the end.

AN ILLUSTRATION TO DANTE

Here are Paolo and Francesca
whirled around in the circle of Hell
clipped serenely together
her dead face raised against his.
I can feel the pressure of his arms
like yours about me, locking.

They float in a sea of whitish blobs –
fire, is it? It could have been
hail, said Ruskin, but Rossetti
'didn't know how to do hail'.
Well, he could do tenderness.
My spine trickles with little white flames.

TOKENS

The sheets have been laundered clean
of our joint essence – a compound,
not a mixture; but here are still

your forgotten pipe and tobacco,
your books open on my table,
your voice speaking in my poems.

NAXAL

The concrete road from the palace to the cinema
bruises the feet. At the Chinese Embassy
I turn past high new walls on to padded mud.
A road is intended – men with trowels and baskets
work on it daily, dreamy Nepali girls
tilt little pots of water on to cement –
but it's gentle walking now. It leads 'inside'.
The tall pine at the end – still notable
though it lost its lingam top for winter firewood –
begins the village: a couple of streets, a temple,
an open space with the pond and the peepul tree,
rows of brick houses, little businesses
proceeding under their doll's-house-level beams;
rice being pounded, charcoal fires in pots,
rickshaws for people like me who don't want them.
The children wave and call 'Bye-bye! Paisa?'
holding out their perfect hands for my coins.
These houses may be eighteenth century:
I covet their fretted lattice window-frames
and stare slightly too long into back rooms.
There are no screens at the carved windows, no filters
for the water they splash and drink at the common pump;
and no mosquitoes now, in the early spring.
But finally, stepping over the warm threshold
of the temple courtyard, I feel a tentative itch;
passing the scummy tank, a little sickness;
touching an infant's head, a little pain.

BODNATH

I have made my pilgrimage a day early:
Ash Wednesday is tomorrow; this week is Losar.
Pacing clockwise around the chaitya
I twirl the prayerwheels, my foreign fingers
polishing their bronze by a fraction more.
The courtyard is crowded with Tibetans,
incredibly jewelled and furred and hatted –
colour-plates from the National Geographic.
The beggar-woman with her monstrous leg
and the snuffling children are genuine too.

I toss them paisa; then go to spend
thirty rupees on a turquoise-studded
silver spoon for the Watkins' baby.

High on his whitewashed mound, Lord Buddha
overlooks the blossom of kite-tails
fluttering from his solid neck.
Om Mani Padme Hum.
His four painted square faces
turn twelve coloured eyes on the globe.
In the shrine below I see him again:
dim bronze, made of curves and surfaces,
shadowed, vulnerable, retiring.
Filmy scarves of white muslin
veil him; rice-grains lie at his feet;
in copper bowls arranged before him
smouldering incense crumbles to ash.

EXTERNAL SERVICE

Already I know my way around the bazaar,
can use half a dozen words of basic Nepali,
and recognize several incarnations of Shiva.
If I stay here much longer I shall learn to identify
more trees besides those in our compound,
other birds than the rock-dove and the crow.
That plink-plink rhythm in the distance is a rice-mill.
The cannon is fired at noon, or to mark a death –
an echoing gesture. Now on the foreign news
I hear that the serious thunder-makers from Ireland
have crossed the channel. A pall of thick black smoke,
says the tidy English voice, hangs over London.
Here the sky is crystal. It is time to go.

FLYING BACK

They give us moistened BOAC towels
and I scrub my forehead. Red powder
for Holi: a trace of Delhi, an assault
met there in the wild streets this morning.

Without compunction I obliterate it –
India's not my country, let it go.
But crumpling the vermilion-stained napkin
(I shan't read it: some priest may do that)
I think of the stone foreheads in their hundreds:
Ganesh and Hanuman, who made me smile,
and Vishnu, and the four faces of Buddha,
reddened with genuine devotions;
and of the wooden cleft in a twisted tree
which I saw a beggar-woman sign scarlet
before she pressed her face down on to it;
and here's Nepal again. Sacred places
don't travel. The gods are stronger at home.
But if my tentative western brow may wear
this reluctant blush, these grains at the hair-roots,
I claim the right also to an image
as guardian; and choose winged Garuda.
His bland archaic countenance beams out
that serenity to which I journey.

NEAR CREESLOUGH

I am in a foreign country.
There are heron and cormorant on the lake.
Young men in T-shirts against an Atlantic gale
are wheeling gravel, renewing the paths
in a stone shell chalked with their own history:

something to fear and covet.
We are the only visitors.
Notices tell us in two old languages
(one mine) that this is Caisleán na dTúath,
Doe Castle. A castle for everyman.

It has ramparts, towers, a dungeon –
we step over gridded emptiness.
The floors have rotted away in seventy years;
the spiral stair endures, a little chipped,
after four hundred. Here is my phobia.

And for you, at the top of it,
yours: a wind-racked vacancy,
a savage drop, a view with no holds –
to which you climb; and if you do, I do:
going up, after all, is the lesser challenge.

The high ledge receives us.
We stand there half a minute longer
than honour and simple vanity require;
then I follow you down the stone gullet,
feet on the splintering treads, eyes inward,

and we step on springy grass
once again; there have been no lapses.
Now ravens ferrying food up to a nest
make their easy ascents. Pleased with our own
we stroll away to eat oranges in the car.

KILMACRENAN

The hailstorm was in my head.
It drove us out into the blind lanes
to stumble over gravel and bog,
teeter on the skidding riverbank
together, stare down and consider.
But we drew back. When the real hail
began its pounding upon us
we were already half recovered.
Walking under that pouring icefall
hand in hand, towards lighted rooms,
we became patchworks of cold and hot,
glowing, streaming with water,
dissolving whatever dared to touch us.

GLENSHANE

Abandoning all my principles
I travel by car with you for days,
eat meat from tins, drink pints of Guinness,
smoke too much, and now on this pass
higher than all our settled landscapes
feed salted peanuts into your mouth
as you drive at eighty miles an hour.

THE INNER HARBOUR

Beginnings

FUTURE WORK

'Please send future work'
                    – Editor's note on a rejection slip.

It is going to be a splendid summer.
The apple tree will be thick with golden russets
expanding weightily in the soft air.
I shall finish the brick wall beside the terrace
and plant out all the geranium cuttings.
Pinks and carnations will be everywhere.

She will come out to me in the garden,
her bare feet pale on the cut grass,
bringing jasmine tea and strawberries on a tray.
I shall be correcting the proofs of my novel
(third in a trilogy – simultaneous publication
in four continents); and my latest play

will be in production at the Aldwych
starring Glenda Jackson and Paul Scofield
with Olivier brilliant in a minor part.
I shall probably have finished my translations
of Persian creation myths and the Pre-Socratics
(drawing new parallels) and be ready to start

on Lucretius. But first I'll take a break
at the chess championships in Manila –
on present form, I'm fairly likely to win.
And poems? Yes, there will certainly be poems:
they sing in my head, they tingle along my nerves.
It is all magnificently about to begin.

OUR TRIP TO THE FEDERATION

We went to Malaya for an afternoon,
driving over the long dull roads
in Bill's Toyota, the two boys in the back.
It was rubber plantations mostly
and villages like all Asian villages,
brown with dust and wood, bright with marketing.

Before we had to turn back we stopped
at a Chinese roadside cemetery
and visited among the long grass
the complicated coloured graves,
patchwork semi-circles of painted stone:
one mustn't set a foot on the wrong bit.

Across the road were rubber trees again
and a kampong behind: we looked in
at thatched houses, flowering shrubs, melons,
unusual speckled poultry, and the usual
beautiful children. We observed
how the bark was slashed for rubber-tapping.

Does it sound like a geography lesson
or a dream? Rubber-seeds are mottled,
smooth, like nuts. I picked up three
and have smuggled them absent-mindedly
in and out of several countries.
Shall I plant them and see what grows?

MR MORRISON

Goslings dive in the lake,
leaves dazzle on the trees;
on the warm grass two ducks are parked neatly
together like a pair of shoes.

A coot plays beaks with its chick;
children laugh and exclaim.
Mr Morrison saunters past, smiling at them,
humming a Sunday-school hymn.

He wonders about his mood,
irredeemably content:
he should worry more about poverty, oppression,
injustice; but he can't, he can't.

He is not too callous to care
but is satisfied in his work,
well-fed, well-housed, tolerably married,
and enjoying a walk in the park.

Then the sun sticks in the sky,
the tune sticks in his throat,
a burning hand with razors for fingernails
reaches inside his coat

and hotly claws at his heart.
He stands very quiet and still,
seeing if he dares to breathe just a fraction;
sweating; afraid he'll fall.

With stiff little wooden steps
he edges his way to a bench
and lowers his body with its secret fiery
tenant down, inch by inch.

He orders himself to be calm:
no doubt it will soon pass.
He resolves to smoke less, watch his cholesterol,
walk more, use the car less.

And it passes: he is released,
the stabbing fingers depart.
Tentatively at first, then easily,
he fills his lungs without hurt.

He is safe; and he is absolved:
it was not just pain, after all;
it enrolled him among the sufferers, allotted him
a stake in the world's ill.

Doors open inside his head;
once again he begins to hum:
he's been granted one small occasion for worry
and the promise of more to come.

THINGS

There are worse things than having behaved foolishly in public.
There are worse things than these miniature betrayals,
committed or endured or suspected; there are worse things
than not being able to sleep for thinking about them.
It is 5 a.m. All the worse things come stalking in
and stand icily about the bed looking worse and worse
                                        and worse.

A WAY OUT

The other option's to become a bird.
That's kindly done, to guess from how they sing,
decently independent of the word
as we are not; and how they use the air
to sail as we might soaring on a swing
higher and higher; but the rope's not there,

it's free fall upward, out into the sky;
or if the arc veer downward, then it's planned:
a bird can loiter, skimming just as high
as lets him supervise the hazel copse,
the turnip field, the orchard, and then land
on just the twig he's chosen. Down he drops

to feed, if so it be: a pretty killer,
a keen-eyed stomach weighted like a dart.
He feels no pity for the caterpillar,
that moistly munching hoop of innocent green.
It is such tender lapses twist the heart.
A bird's heart is a tight little red bean,

untwistable. His beak is made of bone,
his feet apparently of stainless wire;
his coat's impermeable; his nest's his own.
The clogging multiplicity of things
amongst which other creatures, battling, tire
can be evaded by a pair of wings.

68

The point is, most of it occurs below,
earthed at the levels of the grovelling wood
and gritty buildings. Up's the way to go.
If it's escapist, if it's like a dream
the dream's prolonged until it ends for good.
I see no disadvantage in the scheme.

PRELUDE

Is it the long dry grass that is so erotic,
waving about us with hair-fine fronds of straw,
with feathery flourishes of seed, inviting us
to cling together, fall, roll into it
blind and gasping, smothered by stalks and hair,
pollen and each other's tongues on our hot faces?
Then imagine if the summer rain were to come,
heavy drops hissing through the warm air,
a sluice on our wet bodies, plastering us
with strands of delicious grass; a hum in our ears.

We walk a yard apart, talking
of literature and of botany.
We have known each other, remotely, for nineteen years.

ACCIDENTAL

We awakened facing each other
across the white counterpane.
I prefer to be alone in the mornings.
The waiter offered us
melon, papaya, orange juice or fresh raspberries.
We did not discuss it.

All those years of looking but not touching:
at most a kiss in a taxi.
And now this accident,
this blind unstoppable robot walk
into a conspiracy of our bodies.
Had we ruined the whole thing?

The waiter waited:
it was his business to appear composed.
Perhaps we should make it ours also?
We moved an inch or two closer together.
Our toes touched. We looked. We had decided.
Papaya then; and coffee and rolls. Of course.

A MESSAGE

Discreet, not cryptic. I write to you from the garden
in tawny, provoking August; summer is just
on the turn. The lawn is hayseeds and grassy dust.

There are brilliant yellow daisies, though, and fuchsia
(you'll know why) and that mauve and silvery-grey
creeper under the apple tree where we lay.

There have been storms. The apples are few, but heavy,
heavy. And where blossom was, the tree
surges with bright pink flowers – the sweet pea

has taken it over again. Things operate
oddly here. Remember how I found
the buddleia dead, and cut it back to the ground?

That was in April. Now it's ten feet high:
thick straight branches – they've never been so strong –
leaves like a new species, half a yard long,

and spikes of flowers, airily late for their season
but gigantic. A mutation, is it? Well,
summers to come will test it. Let time tell.

Gardens are rife with sermon-fodder. I delve
among blossoming accidents for their designs
but make no statement. Read between these lines.

PROPOSAL FOR A SURVEY

Another poem about a Norfolk church,
a neolithic circle, Hadrian's Wall?
Histories and prehistories: indexes
and bibliographies can't list them all.
A map of Poets' England from the air
could show not only who and when but where.

Aerial photogrammetry's the thing,
using some form of infra-red technique.
Stones that have been so fervently described
surely retain some heat. They needn't speak:
the cunning camera ranging in its flight
will chart their higher temperatures as light.

We'll see the favoured regions all lit up –
the Thames a fiery vein, Cornwall a glow,
Tintagel like an incandescent stud,
most of East Anglia sparkling like Heathrow;
and Shropshire luminous among the best,
with Offa's Dyke in diamonds to the west.

The Lake District will be itself a lake
of patchy brilliance poured along the vales,
with somewhat lesser splashes to the east
across Northumbria and the Yorkshire dales.
Cities and churches, villages and lanes,
will gleam in sparks and streaks and radiant stains.

The lens, of course, will not discriminate
between the venerable and the new;
Stonehenge and Avebury may catch the eye
but Liverpool will have its aura too.
As well as Canterbury there'll be Leeds
and Hull criss-crossed with nets of glittering beads.

Nor will the cool machine be influenced
by literary fashion to reject
any on grounds of quality or taste:
intensity is all it will detect,
mapping in light, for better or for worse,
whatever has been written of in verse.

71

The dreariness of eighteenth-century odes
will not disqualify a crag, a park,
a country residence; nor will the rant
of satirists leave London in the dark.
All will shine forth. But limits there must be:
borders will not be crossed, nor will the sea.·

Let Scotland, Wales and Ireland chart themselves,
as they'd prefer. For us, there's just one doubt:
that medieval England may be dimmed
by age, and all that's earlier blotted out.
X-rays might help. But surely ardent rhyme
will, as it's always claimed, outshine mere time?

By its own power the influence will rise ·
from sites and settlements deep underground
of those who sang about them while they stood.
Pale phosphorescent glimmers will be found
of epics chanted to pre-Roman tunes
and poems in, instead of about, runes.

FAIRY-TALE

This is a story. Dear Clive
(a name unmet among my acquaintance)
you landed on my island: Mauritius
I'll call it – it was not unlike.
The Governor came to meet your plane.
I stood on the grass by the summerhouse.
It was dark, I think. And next morning
we walked in the ripples of the sea
watching the green and purple creatures
flashing in and out of the waves
about our ankles. Seabirds, were they?
Or air-fishes, a flying shoal
of sea-parrots, finned and feathered?
Even they were less of a marvel,
pretty things, than that you'd returned
after a year and such distraction
to walk with me on the splashy strand.

AT THE CREATIVE WRITING COURSE

Slightly frightened of the bullocks
as we walk into their mud towards them
she arms herself by naming them for me:
'Friesian, Aberdeen, Devon, South Devon . . . '
A mixed herd. I was nervous too,
but no longer. 'Devon, Friesian, Aberdeen . . . '
the light young voice chants at them
faster as the long heavy heads
lift and lurch towards us. And pause,
turn away to let us pass. I am learning
to show confidence before large cattle.
She is learning to be a poet.

Endings

THE EX-QUEEN AMONG THE ASTRONOMERS

They serve revolving saucer eyes,
dishes of stars; they wait upon
huge lenses hung aloft to frame
the slow procession of the skies.

They calculate, adjust, record,
watch transits, measure distances.
They carry pocket telescopes
to spy through when they walk abroad.

Spectra possess their eyes; they face
upwards, alert for meteorites,
cherishing little glassy worlds:
receptacles for outer space.

But she, exile, expelled, ex-queen,
swishes among the men of science
waiting for cloudy skies, for nights
when constellations can't be seen.

She wears the rings he let her keep;
she walks as she was taught to walk
for his approval, years ago.
His bitter features taunt her sleep.

And so when these have laid aside
their telescopes, when lids are closed
between machine and sky, she seeks
terrestrial bodies to bestride.

She plucks this one or that among
the astronomers, and is become
his canopy, his occultation;
she sucks at earlobe, penis, tongue

mouthing the tubes of flesh; her hair
crackles, her eyes are comet-sparks.
She brings the distant briefly close
above his dreamy abstract stare.

OFF THE TRACK

Our busy springtime has corrupted
into a green indolence of summer,
static, swollen, invisibly devoured.
Too many leaves have grown between us.
Almost without choosing I have turned
from wherever we were towards this thicket.
It is not the refuge I had hoped for.
Walking away from you I walk
into a trailing mist of caterpillars:
they swing at my face, tinily suspended,
half-blinding; and my hands are smudged
with a syrup of crushed aphids.

You must be miles away by now
in open country, climbing steadily,
head down, looking for larks' eggs.

BEAUX YEUX

Arranging for my due ration of terror
involves me in such lunacies
as recently demanding to be shown
the broad blue ovals of your eyes.

Yes: quite as alarming as you'd promised,
those lapidary iris discs
level in your dark small face.
Still, for an hour or two I held them

until you laughed, replaced your tinted glasses,
switched accents once again
and went away, looking faintly uncertain
in the sunlight (but in charge, no doubt of it)

and leaving me this round baby sparrow
modelled in feather-coloured clay
a small snug handful; hardly apt
unless in being cooler than a pebble.

SEND-OFF

Half an hour before my flight was called
he walked across the airport bar towards me
carrying what was left of our future
together: two drinks on a tray.

IN FOCUS

Inside my closed eyelids, printed out
from some dying braincell as I awakened,
was this close-up of granular earthy dust,
fragments of chaff and grit, a triangular
splinter of glass, a rusty metal washer
on rough concrete under a wooden step.

75

Not a memory. But the caption told me
I was at Grange Farm, seven years old,
in the back yard, kneeling outside the shed
with some obscure seven-year-old's motive,
seeing as once, I must believe, I saw:
sharply; concentrating as once I did.

Glad to be there again I relaxed the focus
(eyes still shut); let the whole scene open out
to the pump and separator under the porch,
the strolling chickens, the pear trees next to the yard,
the barn full of white cats, the loaded haycart,
the spinney . . . I saw it rolling on and on.

As it couldn't, of course. That I had faced
when I made my compulsive return visit
after more than twenty years. 'Your aunt's not well'
said Uncle George – little and gnarled himself –
'You'll find she doesn't talk.' They'd sold the farm,
retired to Melton Mowbray with their daughter.

'Premature senility' she whispered.
But we all went out together in the car
to see the old place, Auntie sitting
straight-backed, dignified, mute,
perhaps a little puzzled as we churned
through splattering clay lanes, between wet hedges

to Grange Farm again: to a square house,
small, bleak, and surrounded by mud;
to be greeted, shown to the parlour, given tea,
with Auntie's affliction gently signalled –
'Her mouth hurts.' Not my real aunt,
nor my real uncle. Both dead now.

I find it easiest to imagine dying
as like the gradual running down of a film,
the brain still flickering when the heart and blood
have halted, and the last few frames
lingering. Then where the projector jams
is where we go, or are, or are no longer.

If that comes anywhere near it, then I hope
that for those two an after-image glowed
in death of something better than mud and silence
or than my minute study of a patch of ground;
unless, like that for me, it spread before them
sunny ploughland, pastures, the scented orchard.

LETTER FROM HIGHGATE WOOD

Your 'wedge of stubborn particles':

that silver birch, thin as a bent flagpole,
drives up through elm and oak and hornbeam
to sky-level, catching the late sunlight.

There's woodsmoke, a stack of cut billets
from some thick trunk they've had to hack;
and of course a replacement programme under way –
saplings fenced off against marauders.

'We have seasons' your poem says;
and your letter tells me the black invader
has moved into the lymph; is not defeated.

'He's lucky to be still around' said your friend –
himself still around, still travelling
after a near-axing as severe,
it yet may prove, as yours at present.

I have come here to think, not for comfort;
to confront these matters, to imagine
the proliferating ungentle cells.

But the place won't let me be fearful;
the green things work their usual trick –
'Choose life' – and I remember instead
our own most verdant season.

My dear, after more than a dozen years
light sings in the leaves of it still.

POEM ENDED BY A DEATH

They will wash all my kisses and fingerprints off you
and my tearstains – I was more inclined to weep
in those wild-garlicky days – and our happier stains,
thin scales of papery silk . . . Fuck that for a cheap
opener; and false too – any such traces
you pumiced away yourself, those years ago
when you sent my letters back, in the week I married
that anecdotal ape. So start again. So:

They will remove the tubes and drips and dressings
which I censor from my dreams. They will, it is true,
wash you; and they will put you into a box.
After which whatever else they may do
won't matter. This is my laconic style.
You praised it, as I praised your intricate pearled
embroideries; these links laced us together,
plain and purl across the ribs of the world . . .

HAVING NO MIND FOR THE SAME POEM

Nor for the same conversation again and again.
But the power of meditation to cure an allergy,
that I will discuss
cross-legged on the lawn at evening
midges flittering, a tree beside us
none of us can name;
and rocks; a scent of syringa;
certain Japanese questions; the journey . . .

Nor for parody.

Nor, if we come to it, for the same letter:
'hard to believe . . . I remember best his laugh . . .
such a vigorous man . . . please tell . . . '
and running, almost running to stuff coins
into the box for cancer research.

The others.

Nor for the same hopeless prayer.

SYRINGA

The syringa's out. That's nice for me:
all along Charing Cross Embankment
the sweet dragging scent reinventing
one of my childhood gardens.
Nice for the drunks and drop-outs too,
if they like it. I'm walking to work:
they'll be here all day under the blossom
with their cider and their British sherry
and their carrier-bags of secrets.
There's been a change in the population:
the ones I had names for – Fat Billy,
the Happy Couple, the Lady with the Dog –
have moved on or been moved off.
But it doesn't do to wonder:
staring hurts in two directions. Once
a tall man chased me here, and I ran
for no good reason: afraid, perhaps,
of turning into Mrs Toothless
with her ankle-socks and her pony-tailed skull
whose eyes avoided mine so many mornings.
And she's gone too. The place has been,
as whatever office will have termed it,
cleaned up. Except that it's not clean
and not really a place: a hesitation
between the traffic fumes and a fragrance,
where this evening I shall walk again.

The Thing Itself

DRY SPELL

It is not one thing, but more one thing than others:
the carved spoon broken in its case, a slate split on the roof,
dead leaves falling upon dead grass littered
with feathers, and the berries ripe too soon.

All of a piece and all in pieces, the dry mouth failing
to say it. I am sick with symbols.
Here is the thing itself: it is a drought.
I must learn it and live it drably through.

79

VISITED

This truth-telling is well enough
looking into the slaty eyes of the visitants
acknowledging the messages they bring

but they plod past so familiarly
mouldy faces droning about acceptance
that one almost looks for a real monster

spiny and gaping as the fine mad fish
in the corner of that old shipwreck painting
rearing its red gullet out of the foam.

THE SOHO HOSPITAL FOR WOMEN

I

Strange room, from this angle:
white door open before me,
strange bed, mechanical hum, white lights.
There will be stranger rooms to come.

As I almost slept I saw the deep flower opening
and leaned over into it, gratefully.
It swimmingly closed in my face. I was not ready.
It was not death, it was acceptance.

*

Our thin patient cat died purring,
her small triangular head tilted back,
the nurse's fingers caressing her throat,
my hand on her shrunken spine; the quick needle.

That was the second death by cancer.
The first is not for me to speak of.
It was telephone calls and brave letters
and a friend's hand bleeding under the coffin.

*

Doctor, I am not afraid of a word.
But neither do I wish to embrace that visitor,
to engulf it as Hine-Nui-te-Po
engulfed Maui; that would be the way of it.

And she was the winner there: her womb crushed him.
Goddesses can do these things.
But I have admitted the gloved hands and the speculum
and must part my ordinary legs to the surgeon's knife.

2

Nellie has only one breast
ample enough to make several.
Her quilted dressing-gown softens
to semi-doubtful this imbalance
and there's no starched vanity
in our abundant ward-mother:
her silvery hair's in braids, her slippers
loll, her weathered smile holds true.
When she dresses up in her black
with her glittering marcasite brooch on
to go for the weekly radium treatment
she's the bright star of the taxi-party –
whatever may be growing under her ribs.

*

Doris hardly smokes in the ward –
and hardly eats more than a dreamy spoonful –
but the corridors and bathrooms
reek of her Players Number 10,
and the drug-trolley pauses
for long minutes by her bed.
Each week for the taxi-outing
she puts on her skirt again
and has to pin the slack waistband
more tightly over her scarlet sweater.
Her face, a white shadow through smoked glass,
lets Soho display itself unregarded.

*

Third in the car is Mrs Golding
who never smiles. And why should she?

3

The senior consultant on his rounds
murmurs in so subdued a voice
to the students marshalled behind
that they gather in, forming a cell,
a cluster, a rosette around him
as he stands at the foot of my bed
going through my notes with them,
half-audibly instructive, grave.

The slight ache as I strain forward
to listen still seems imagined.

Then he turns his practised smile on me:
'How are you this morning?' 'Fine,
very well, thank you.' I smile too.
And possibly all that murmurs within me
is the slow dissolving of stitches.

4

I am out in the supermarket choosing –
this very afternoon, this day –
picking up tomatoes, cheese, bread,

things I want and shall be using
to make myself a meal, while they
eat their stodgy suppers in bed:

Janet with her big freckled breasts,
her prim Scots voice, her one friend,
and never in hospital before,

who came in to have a few tests
and now can't see where they'll end;
and Coral in the bed by the door

who whimpered and gasped behind a screen
with nurses to and fro all night
and far too much of the day;

pallid, bewildered, nineteen.
And Mary, who will be all right
but gradually. And Alice, who may.

Whereas I stand almost intact,
giddy with freedom, not with pain.
I lift my light basket, observing

how little I needed in fact;
and move to the checkout, to the rain,
to the lights and the long street curving.

VARIATIONS ON A THEME OF HORACE

Clear is the man and of a cold life
who needn't fear the slings and arrows;
cold is the man, and perhaps the moorish bows
will avoid him and the wolf turn tail.

*

Sitting in the crypt under bare arches
at a quite ordinary table with a neat cloth,
a glass of wine before him, 'I'm never sure'
he said 'that I'll wake up tomorrow morning.'

Upstairs musicians were stretching their bows
for a late quartet which would also save us from nothing.
This ex-church was bombed to rubble,
rebuilt. It is not of that he was thinking.

And policemen decorate the underground stations
to protect us from the impure of heart;
the traveller must learn to suspect his neighbour,
each man his own watchdog. Nor of that.

Of a certain high felicity, perhaps,
imagining its absence; of the chances.
(If echoes fall into the likeness of music
that, like symmetry, may be accidental.)

'Avoid archaism for its own sake –
viols, rebecks: what is important
is simply that the instruments should be able
to play the notes.' A hard-learnt compromise.

But using what we have while we have it
seems, at times, enough or more than enough.
And here were old and newer things for our pleasure –
the sweet curves of the arches; music to come.

Which this one set before him with his own death –
far from probably imminent, not soon likely –
ticking contrapuntally like a pace-maker
inside him. Were we, then, lighter, colder?

Had we ignored a central insistent theme?
Possibly even the birds aren't happy:
it may be that they twitter from rage or fear.
So many tones; one can't be sure of one's reading.

Just as one can't quite despise Horace
on whom the dreaded tree never did quite fall;
timid enjoyer that he was, he died
in due course of something or other. And meanwhile

sang of his Lalage in public measures,
enjoyed his farm and his dinners rather more,
had as much, no doubt, as any of us to lose.
And the black cypress stalks after us all.

A WALK IN THE SNOW

Neighbours lent her a tall feathery dog
to make her expedition seem natural.
She couldn't really fancy a walk alone,
drawn though she was to the shawled whiteness,
the flung drifts of wool. She was not a walker.
Her winter pleasures were in firelit rooms –
entertaining friends with inventive dishes
or with sherry, conversation, palm-reading:
'You've suffered' she'd say. 'Of course, life is suffering . . . '
holding a wrist with her little puffy hand
older than her face. She was writing a novel.
But today there was the common smothered in snow,
blanked-out, white as meringue, the paths gone:
a few mounds of bracken spikily veiled
and the rest smooth succulence. They pocked it,

she and the dog; they wrote on it with their feet –
her suede boots, his bright flurrying paws.
It was their snow, and they took it.
                                    That evening
the poltergeist, the switcher-on of lights
and conjuror with ashtrays, was absent.
The house lay mute. She hesitated a moment
at bedtime before the Valium bottle;
then, to be on the safe side, took her usual;
and swam into a deep snowy sleep
where a lodge (was it?) and men in fur hats,
and the galloping . . . and something about . . .

A DAY IN OCTOBER

1.30 p.m.
Outside the National Gallery
a man checks bags for bombs or weapons –
not thoroughly enough: he'd have missed
a tiny hand-grenade in my make-up purse,
a cigarette packet of gelignite.
I walk in gently to Room III
not to disturb them: Piero's angels,
serene and cheerful, whom surely nothing could frighten,
and St Michael in his red boots
armed against all comers.
Brave images. But under my heart
an explosive bubble of tenderness gathers
and I shiver before the chalky Christ:
what must we do to save
the white limbs, pale tree, trusting verticals?
Playing the old bargaining game
I juggle with prices, offer a finger
for this or that painting, a hand or an eye
for the room's contents. What for the whole building?
And shouldn't I jump aside if the bomb flew,
cowardly as instinct makes us?
'Goodbye' I tell the angels, just in case.

4 p.m.
It's a day for pictures:
this afternoon, in the course of duty,
I open a book of black-and-white photographs,
rather smudgy, the text quaintly translated
from the Japanese: Atomic Bomb Injuries.
All the familiar shots are here:
the shadow blast-printed on to a wall,
the seared or bloated faces of children.
I am managing not to react to them.
Then this soldier, who died from merely helping,
several slow weeks afterwards.
His body is a Scarfe cartoon –
skinny trunk, enormous toes and fingers,
joints huge with lymphatic nodes.
My throat swells with tears at last.
Almost I fall into that inheritance,
long resisted and never my own doctrine,
a body I would not be part of.
I all but say it: 'What have we done?
How shall we pay for this?'
But having a job to do I swallow
tears, guilt, these pallid secretions;
close the book; and carry it away
to answer someone's factual enquiry.

7 p.m.
In the desert the biggest tank battle
since World War II smashes on.
My friends are not sure whether their brothers
in Israel are still alive.
All day the skies roar with jets.
And I do not write political poems.

86

HOUSE-TALK

Through my pillow, through mattress, carpet, floor and ceiling,
sounds ooze up from the room below:
footsteps, chinking crockery, hot-water pipes groaning,
the muffled clunk of the refrigerator door,
and voices. They are trying to be quiet,
my son and his friends, home late in the evening.

Tones come softly filtered through the layers of padding.
I hear the words but not what the words are,
as on my radio when the batteries are fading.
Voices are reduced to a muted music:
Andrew's bass, his friend's tenor, the indistinguishable
light murmurs of the girls; occasional giggling.

Surely wood and plaster retain something
in their grain of all the essences they absorb?
This house has been lived in for ninety years,
nine by us. It has heard all manner of talking.
Its porous fabric must be saturated
with words. I offer it my peaceful breathing.

FOREIGNER

These winds bully me:

I am to lie down in a ditch
quiet under the thrashing nettles
and pull the mud up to my chin.

Not that I would submit so
to one voice only;
but by the voices of these several winds
merged into a flowing fringe of tones
that swirl and comb over the hills
I am compelled.

I shall lie sound-proofed in the mud,
a huge caddis-fly larva,
a face floating upon Egyptian unguents
in a runnel at the bottom of England.

IN THE DINGLE PENINSULA

We give ten pence to the old woman
and climb through nettles to the beehive hut.
You've been before. You're showing me prehistory,
ushering me into a stone cocoon.
I finger the corbelled wall and squat against it
bowing my back in submission to its curves.

The floor's washed rock: not even a scorchmark
as trace of the once-dwellers. But they're here,
closer than you, and trying to seduce me:
the arched stones burn against my shoulders,
my knees tingle, the cool air buzzes . . .
I drag my eyelids open and sleep-walk out.

'We're skeletons underneath' I've heard you say,
looking into coffins at neat arrangements
laid out in museums. We're skeletons.
I take the bones of your hand lightly in mine
through the dry flesh and walk unresisting,
willing to share it, over the peopled soil.

IN THE TERAI

Our throats full of dust, teeth harsh with it,
plastery sweat in our hair and nostrils,
we slam the flaps of the Landrover down
and think we choke on these roads.
Well, they will be better in time:
all along the dry riverbed
just as when we drove past this morning
men and women squatting under umbrellas
or cloth stretched over sticks, or nothing,
are splitting chipped stones to make smaller chips,
picking the fingernail-sized fragments
into graded heaps: roads by the handful.
We stop at the village and buy glasses of tea,
stewed and sweet; swallow dust with it
and are glad enough. The sun tilts lower.
Somewhere, surely, in this valley
under cool thatch mothers are feeding children

with steamy rice, leaning over them
to pour milk or water; the cups
tasting of earthenware, neutral, clean,
the young heads smelling only of hair.

RIVER

' . . . I saw with infinite pleasure the great object of my
mission; the long sought for, majestic Niger, glittering
to the morning sun, as broad as the Thames at West-
minster, and flowing slowly *to the eastward.*'
— Mungo Park: *Travels in the Interior Districts of Africa.*

The strong image is always the river
was a line for the poem I never wrote
twenty years ago and never have written
of the green Wanganui under its willows
or the ice-blue milky-foaming Clutha
stopping my tremulous teenage heart.

But now when I cross Westminster Bridge
all that comes to mind is the Niger
a river Mungo Park invented for me
as he invented all those African villages
and a certain kind of astonishing silence –
the explorer having done the poet's job
and the poet feeling gratefully redundant.

To and Fro

THE INNER HARBOUR

Paua-Shell

Spilt petrol
oil on a puddle
the sea's colour-chart
porcelain, tie-dyed.
Tap the shell:
glazed calcium.

89

Cat's-Eye

Boss-eye, wall-eye, squinty lid
stony door for a sea-snail's tunnel

the long beach littered with them
domes of shell, discarded virginities

where the green girl wanders, willing
to lose hers to the right man

or to the wrong man, if he should raise
his frolic head above a sand dune

glossy-black-haired, and that smile on him

Sea-Lives

Under the sand at low tide
are whispers, hisses, long slithers,
bubbles, the suck of ingestion, a soft
snap: mysteries and exclusions.

Things grow on the dunes too –
pale straggle of lupin-bushes,
cutty-grass, evening primroses
puckering in the low light.

But the sea knows better.
Walk at the edge of its rich waves:
on the surface nothing shows;
underneath it is fat and fecund.

Shrimping-Net

Standing just under the boatshed
knee-deep in dappled water
sand-coloured legs and the sand itself
greenish in the lit ripples
watching the shrimps avoid her net
little flexible glass rockets
and the lifted mesh always empty
gauze and wire dripping sunlight

She is too tall to stand under
this house. It is a fantasy

And moving in from the bright outskirts
further under the shadowy floor
hearing a footstep creak above
her head brushing the rough timber
edging further bending her knees
creosote beams grazing her shoulder
the ground higher the roof lower
sand sifting on to her hair

She kneels in dark shallow water,
palms pressed upon shells and weed.

IMMIGRANT

November '63: eight months in London.
I pause on the low bridge to watch the pelicans:
they float swanlike, arching their white necks
over only slightly ruffled bundles of wings,
burying awkward beaks in the lake's water.

I clench cold fists in my Marks and Spencer's jacket
and secretly test my accent once again:
St James's Park; St James's Park; St James's Park.

SETTLERS

First there is the hill   wooden houses
warm branches close against the face

Bamboo was in it somewhere
or another tall reed   and pines

Let it shift a little
settle into its own place

When we lived on the mountain
she said   But it was not
a mountain   nor they placed so high
nor where they came from a mountain
Manchester   and then the slow seas
hatches battened   a typhoon
so that all in the end became
mountains
        Steps to the venture
vehicles luggage bits of paper
all their people fallen away
shrunken into framed wedding groups
One knows at the time it can't be happening

Neighbours helped them build a house
what neighbours there were   and to farm
she and the boy much alone
her husband away in the town working
clipping hair   Her heart was weak
they said   ninety years with a weak heart
and such grotesque accidents
burns wrenches caustic soda
conspired against she had to believe

The waterfall   that was real
but she never mentioned the waterfall

After twelve years the slow reverse
from green wetness   cattle   weather
to somewhere at least   a township
air lower than the mountain's   calmer
a house with an orchard   peach and plum trees
tomato plants   their bruised scented leaves

and a third life   grandchildren
even the trip back to England at last

Then calmer still and closer in
suburbs   retraction into a city

We took her a cake for her birthday
going together   it was easier
Separately would have been kinder
and twice   For the same stories

rain cold now on the southerly harbour
wondering she must have been why
alone in the house or whether alone
her son in Europe   but someone
a man she thought in the locked room
where their things were stored   her things
about her   china the boxwood cabinet
photographs   Them's your Grandpa's people
and the noises in the room   a face

Hard to tell if she was frightened

Not simple   no   Much neglected
and much here omitted   Footnotes
Alice and her children gone ahead
the black sheep brother   the money
the whole slow long knotted tangle

And her fine straight profile too
her giggle   Eee   her dark eyes

GOING BACK

There were always the places I couldn't spell, or couldn't find
                                              on maps –
too small, but swollen in family legend:
famous for bush-fires, near-drownings, or just the standard pioneer
grimness – twenty cows to milk by hand
before breakfast, and then a five-mile walk to school.
(Do I exaggerate? Perhaps; but hardly at all.)

They were my father's, mostly. One or two, until I was five,
rolled in and out of my own vision:
a wall with blackboards; a gate where I swung, the wind bleak
                                              in the telegraph wires;
Mother in this or that schoolhouse kitchen,
singing. And, in between, back to familiar bases:
Drury again, Christmas Days in grandparents' houses.

Suddenly no more New Zealand except in receding pictures
for years. And then we had it again, but different:
a city, big schools, my father a university teacher now.
But, being a nostalgic family, we went
in a newish car, along better roads, where once we'd rattled
in the Baby Austin over metal or clay surfaces, unsealed.

And we got most of it – nearly all the places that seemed to matter:
'Do you remember this path?' and 'There's the harbour
we had to cross in the launch when you were a new baby
and a storm came up, and we thought we'd go under.'
Here and there a known vista or the familiar angle
of a room to a garden made my own memories tingle.

But nostalgia-time ran out as I grew older and more busy
and became a parent myself, and left the country
for longer than they had left it; with certain things undone:
among them, two holes in the map empty.
Now I've stitched them in. I have the fabric complete,
the whole of the North Island pinned out flat.

First my own most haunting obsession, the school at Tokorangi.
It was I who spotted the turning off the road,
identified the trees, the mound, the contours programmed into
                                                    my system
when I was five, and the L-shaped shed
echoing for two of us with voices; for the rest
an object of polite historical interest.

And a week later, one for my father, smaller and more remote,
a square wooden box on a little hill.
The door creaked rustily open. He stood in the entrance porch,
                                                    he touched
the tap he'd so often turned, the very nail
where sixty years ago the barometer had hung
to be read at the start of each patterned morning.

Two bits of the back-blocks, then, two differently rural settings
for schools, were they? Schools no longer.
Left idle by the motorized successors of the pioneers
each had the same still mask to offer:
broken windows, grassy silence, all the children gone away,
and classrooms turned into barns for storing hay.

INSTEAD OF AN INTERVIEW

The hills, I told them; and water, and the clear air
(not yielding to more journalistic probings);
and a river or two, I could say, and certain bays
and ah, those various and incredible hills . . .

And all my family still in the one city
within walking distances of each other
through streets I could follow blind. My school was gone
and half my Thorndon smashed for the motorway
but every corner revealed familiar settings
for the dreams I'd not bothered to remember –
ingrained; ingrown; incestuous: like the country.

And another city offering me a lover
and quite enough friends to be going on with;
bookshops; galleries; gardens; fish in the sea;
lemons and passionfruit growing free as the bush.
Then the bush itself; and the wild grand south;
and wooden houses in occasional special towns.

And not a town or a city I could live in.
Home, as I explained to a weeping niece,
home is London; and England, Ireland, Europe.
I have come home with a suitcase full of stones –
of shells and pebbles, pottery, pieces of bark:
here they lie around the floor of my study
as I telephone a cable 'Safely home'

and moments later, thinking of my dears,
wish the over-resonant word cancelled:
'Arrived safely' would have been clear enough,
neutral, kinder. But another loaded word
creeps up now to interrogate me.
By going back to look, after thirteen years,
have I made myself for the first time an exile?

LONDONER

Scarcely two hours back in the country
and I'm shopping in East Finchley High Road
in a cotton skirt, a cardigan, jandals –
or flipflops as people call them here,
where February's winter. Aren't I cold?
The neighbours in their overcoats are smiling
at my smiles and not at my bare toes:
they know me here.
                        I hardly know myself,
yet. It takes me until Monday evening,
walking from the office after dark
to Westminster Bridge. It's cold, it's foggy,
the traffic's as abominable as ever,
and there across the Thames is County Hall,
that uninspired stone body, floodlit.
It makes me laugh. In fact, it makes me sing.

TO MARILYN FROM LONDON

You did London early, at nineteen:
the basement room, the geriatric nursing,
cinema queues, modish fall-apart dresses,
and marriage at Stoke Newington Registry Office,
Spring 1955, on the rebound.

Marrying was what we did in those days.
And soon enough you were back in Wellington
with your eye-shadow and your Edith Piaf records
buying kitchen furniture on hire-purchase
and writing novels when the babies were asleep.

Somehow you're still there, I'm here; and now
Sarah arrives: baby-faced like you then,
second of your four blonde Christmas-tree fairies,
nineteen; competent; with her one suitcase
and her two passports. It begins again.

BELOW LOUGHRIGG

BELOW LOUGHRIGG

The power speaks only out of sleep and blackness
no use looking for the sun
what is not present cannot be illumined

Katherine's lungs, remember, eaten by disease
but Mary's fingers too
devoured and she goes on writing

The water speaks from the rocks, the cavern speaks,
where water halloos through it
this happens also in darkness

A steep bit here, up from the valley
to the terraces, the path eroded by water
Now listen for the voice

These things wane with the vital forces
he said, little having waned in him
except faith, and anger had replaced it

One force can be as good as another
we may not think so; but channelled
in ways it has eaten out; issuing

into neither a pool nor the sea
but a shapely lake afloat with wooded islands
a real water and multiplied on maps

which can be read in the sunlight; for the sun
will not be stopped from visiting
and the lake exists and the wind sings over it.

THREE RAINBOWS IN ONE MORNING

It is not only the eye that is astonished.

Predictable enough in rainbow weather,
the drenched air saturated with colours,
that over each valley should hang an arc
and over this long lake the longest.

Knowing how it happens is no defence.
They stop the car and are delighted.

But some centre of gravity is upset,
some internal gauge or indicator
fed once again with the routine question
'This place, now: would it be possible
to live here?' buzzes, rolls
and registers 'Yes. Yes; perhaps.'

BINOCULARS

'What are you looking at?' 'Looking.'
High screed sides; possibly a raven,
he thought. Bracken a fuzz of rust
on the iron slopes of the fell
(off the edge of their map, nameless)
and the sky clean after rain.
At last he put the binoculars down,
drove on further to the north.

It was a good day in the end:
the cold lake lapping against pines,
and the square-built northern town idle
in sunlight. It seemed they had crossed borders.
Driving south became a return
to nests of trees in ornamental colours.
Leaving, he left her the binoculars
to watch her wrens and robins until spring.

PATHS

I am the dotted lines on the map:
footpaths exist only when they are walked on.
I am gravel tracks through woodland; I am
field paths, the muddy ledge by the stream,
the stepping-stones. I am the grassy lane
open between waist-high bracken where sheep
fidget. I am the track to the top
skirting and scaling rocks. I am the cairn.

Here on the brow of the world I stop,
set my stone face to the wind, and turn
to each wide quarter. I am that I am.

MID-POINT

Finding I've walked halfway around Loughrigg
I wonder: do I still want to go on?
Normally, yes. But now, hardly recovered
from 'flu, and feeling slightly faint in the sun,
dazzled by early spring, I hesitate.
How far is it around this sprawling fell?
I've come perhaps three miles. Will it be four,
or less, the Grasmere way? It's hard to tell.
The ups and downs undo one's feel for distance;
the soaring views distract from what's at hand.
But here's the tarn, spangled with quick refractions
of sunlight, to remind me where I stand.
There's no way on or back except by walking
and whichever route I choose involves a climb.
On, then, no question: if I find myself
lacking in energy, at least I've time.
It will be cooler when I'm facing north –
frost often lingers there – and I'll take heart
from gazing down again on Rydal Water.
The point of no return was at the start.

THE SPIRIT OF THE PLACE

Mist like evaporating stone
smudges the bracken. Not much further now.
Below on the other side of the village
Windermere tilts its pewter face
over towards me as I move downhill.
I've walked my boots clean in gravelly streams;
picking twigs of glittering holly
to take home I've lacerated my fingers
(it serves me right: holly belongs on trees).
Now as the early dusk descends behind me
dogs in the kennels above Nook Lane
are barking, growling, hysterical at something;
and from the housing estate below
a deep mad voice bellows 'Wordsworth! Wordsworth!'

THE VALE OF GRASMERE

These coloured slopes ought to inspire,
as much as anything, discretion:
think of the egotisms laid bare,
the shy campaigns of self-projection
tricked out as visits to Dove Cottage
tellingly rendered. Every year
some poet comes on pilgrimage
along these valleys. Read his verses:
each bud of delicate perception
sprouts from a blossoming neurosis
too well watered by Grasmere –
in which he sees his own reflection.
He sits beside a tarn or ghyll
sensitively eating chocolate
and eyes Helm Crag or Rydal Fell
plotting some novel way to use it.
Most of the rocks are wreathed by now
with faded rags of fluttering soul.
But the body finds another function
for crags and fells, as Wordsworth knew
himself: they offer hands and feet
their own creative work to do.
'I climb because I can't write'
one honest man said. Better so.

LETTER TO ALISTAIR CAMPBELL

Those thorn-trees in your poems, Alistair,
we have them here. Also the white cauldron,
the basin of your waterfall. I stare
at Stock Ghyll Force and can't escape your words.
You'd love this place: it's your Central Otago
in English dress – the bony land's the same;
and if the Cromwell Gorge is doomed to go
under a lake, submerging its brave orchards
for cheap electric power, this is where
you'd find a subtly altered image of it,
its cousin in another hemisphere:
the rivers gentler, hills more widely splayed
but craggy enough. Well. Some year you'll manage
to travel north, as I two years ago
went south. Meanwhile our sons are of an age
to do it for us: Andrew's been with you
in Wellington. Now I'm about to welcome
our firstborn Gregory to England. Soon,
if Andrew will surrender him, he'll come
from grimy fetid London — still my base,
I grant you, still my centre, but with air
that chokes me now each time I enter it –
to this pure valley where no haze but weather
obscures the peaks from time to time, clean rain
or tender mist (forgive my lyrical
effusiveness: Wordsworthian locutions
are carried on the winds in what I call
my this year's home. You've had such fits yourself.)
So: Gregory will come to Ambleside
and see the lakes, the Rothay, all these waters.
Two years ago he sat with me beside
the Clutha, on those rocks where you and I
did our first timid courting. Symmetry
pleases me; correspondences and chimes
are not just ornament. And if I try
too hard to emphasize the visual echoes
between a place of mine and one of yours
it's not only for art's sake but for friendship:
five years of marriage, twenty of divorce
are our foundation. It occurred to me
in August, round about the twenty-third,
that we'd deprived ourselves of cake, champagne,

a silver tea-service, the family gathered –
I almost felt I ought to send a card.
Well, that can wait: it won't be long before
you have my blessings on your twentieth year
with Meg; but let this, in the meantime, be for
our older link through places and your poems.

DECLENSIONS

Snow on the tops: half the day I've sat at the window
   staring at fells made suddenly remote
by whiteness that disguises them as high mountains
   reared behind the bracken-covered slopes
of others whose colour yesterday was theirs.
   In the middle distance, half-stripped trees
have shed pink stains on the grass beneath them.
   That other pinkness over Windermere
is the setting sun through cloud. And in the foreground
   birds act out their various natures
around the food I've set on the terrace wall:
   the plump chaffinch eats on steadily
even in a hail-shower; tits return when it's over
   to swing on their bacon-rind; a dunnock hops
picking stray seeds; and the territorial robin,
   brisk, beady eyed, sees them all off.
I am not at all sure that this is the real world
   but I am looking at it very closely.
Is landscape serious? Are birds? But they are fading
   in dusk, in the crawling darkness. Enough.
Knowing no way to record what is famous
   precisely for being unrecordable,
I draw the curtains and settle to my book:
   Dr William Smith's First Greek Course,
Exercise Fourteen: third declension nouns.
   My letters, awkward from years of non-use,
sprinkle over the page like birds' footprints,
   quaint thorny symbols, pecked with accents:
as I turn the antique model sentences:
   The vines are praised by the husbandmen.
The citizens delight in strife and faction.
   The harbour has a difficult entrance.

WEATHERING

Literally thin-skinned, I suppose, my face
catches the wind off the snow-line and flushes
with a flush that will never wholly settle. Well:
that was a metropolitan vanity,
wanting to look young for ever, to pass.

I was never a pre-Raphaelite beauty,
nor anything but pretty enough to satisfy
men who need to be seen with passable women.
But now that I am in love with a place
which doesn't care how I look, or if I'm happy,

happy is how I look, and that's all.
My hair will turn grey in any case,
my nails chip and flake, my waist thicken,
and the years work all their usual changes.
If my face is to be weather-beaten as well

that's little enough lost, a fair bargain
for a year among lakes and fells, when simply
to look out of my window at the high pass
makes me indifferent to mirrors and to what
my soul may wear over its new complexion.

GOING OUT FROM AMBLESIDE

I

He is lying on his back watching a kestrel,
his head on the turf, hands under his neck,
warm air washing over his face,
and the sky clear blue where the kestrel hovers.

A person comes with a thermometer.
He watches a ceiling for three minutes.
The person leaves. He watches the kestrel again,
his head pressed back among the harebells.

2

Today he will go over to Langdale.
He springs lightly in his seven-league boots
around the side of Loughrigg
bouncing from rock to rock in the water-courses
evading slithery clumps of weed, skipping
like a sheep among the rushes
coursing along the curved path upward
through bracken, over turf to a knoll
and across it, around and on again
higher and higher, glowing with exaltation
up to where it all opens out.
That was easy. And it was just the beginning.

3

They bring him tea or soup.
He does not notice it. He is busy
identifying fungi in Skelghyll Wood,
comparing them with the pictures in his mind:
Purple Blewit, Yellow Prickle Fungus,
Puffball, Russula, two kinds of Boletus –
the right weather for them.
And what are these little pearly knobs
pressing up among the leaf-mould?
He treads carefully over damp grass,
patches of brilliant moss, pine-needles,
hoping for a Fly Agaric.
Scarlet catches his eye. But it was only
reddening leaves on a bramble.
And here's bracken, fully brown,
and acorns. It must be October.

4

What is this high wind coming,
leaves leaping from the trees to bite his face?
A storm. He should have noticed the signs.
But it doesn't matter. Ah, turn into it,
let the rain bite on the warm skin too.

5

Cold. Suddenly cold. Or hot.
A pain under his breastbone;
and his feet are bare. This is curious.

Someone comes with an injection.

6

They have brought Kurt Schwitters to see him,
a clumsy-looking man in a beret
asking for bits of stuff to make a collage.
Here, take my stamp-collection
and the letters my children wrote from school
and this photograph of my wife. She's dead now.
You are dead too, Kurt Schwitters.

7

This is a day for sailing, perhaps,
coming down from the fells to lake-level;
or for something gentler: for idling
with a fishing-line and listening to water;
or just for lying in a boat
on a summer evening in the lee of a shore
letting the wind steer, leaving the hull
to its own course, the waves to lap it along.

8

But where now suddenly? Dawn light,
peaks around him, shadowy and familiar,
tufts of mist over a tarn below.
Somehow he is higher than he intended;
and careless, giddy, running to the edge
and over it, straight down on splintery scree
leaning back on his boots, a ski-run
scattering chips of slate, a skid with no stopping
down through the brief mist and into the tarn.

9

Tomorrow perhaps he will think about Helvellyn . . .

NEW POEMS

IN THE UNICORN, AMBLESIDE

I want to have ice-skates and a hoop
and to have lived all my life in the same house
above Stock; and to skate on Lily Tarn
every winter, because it always freezes –
or always did freeze when you were a girl.

I want to believe your tales about Wordsworth –
'Listen to what the locals say' you tell me:
'He drank in every pub from here to Ullswater,
and had half the girls. We all know that.'
I want not to know better, out of books.

I sit in the pub with my posh friends, talking
literature and publishing as usual.
Some of them really do admire Wordsworth.
But they won't listen to you. I listen:
how can I get you to listen to me?

I can't help not being local;
but I'm here, aren't I? And this afternoon
Jane and I sat beside Lily Tarn
watching the bright wind attack the ice.
None of you were up there skating.

DOWNSTREAM

Last I became a raft of green bubbles
meshed into the miniature leaves
of that small pondweed (has it a name?)
that lies green-black on the stream's face:
a sprinkle of round seeds, if you mistake it,
or of seed-hulls holding air among them.

I was those globules; there they floated –
all there was to do was to float
on the degenerate stream, suburbanized,
the mill-stream where it is lost among houses
and hardly moving, swilling just a little
to and fro if the wind blows it.

But it did move, and I moved on, drifting
until I entered the river
where I was comported upon a tear's fashion
blending into the long water
until you would not see that there had been
tear or bubble or any round thing ever.

THE HILLSIDE

Tawny-white as a ripe hayfield.
But it is heavy with frost, not seed.

It frames him for you as he sits by the window,
his hair white also, a switch of silver.

He pours you another glass of wine,
laughs at your shy anecdotes, quietly caps them,

is witty as always; glows as hardly ever,
his back to the rectangles of glass.

The snow holds off. Clouds neither pass nor lower
their flakes on to the hill's pale surface.

Tell him there is green beneath it still:
he will almost, for this afternoon, believe you.

THIS UNGENTLE MUSIC

Angry Mozart: the only kind for now.
Tinkling would appal on such an evening,
summer, when the possible things to do
are: rip all weeds out of the garden,
butcher the soft redundancy of the hedge
in public; and go, when the light slackens,
to stamp sharp echoes along the street

mouthing futilities: 'A world where . . . '
as if there were a choice of other worlds
than this one in which it is the case
that nothing can stamp out leukaemia.
So Malcolm has had to die at twenty,
humming off on a low blue flame
of heroin, a terminal kindness.

Wild rock howls on someone's record.
Fog sifts over the young moon.

THE RING

Then in the end she didn't marry him
and go to Guyana; the politics of the thing
had to be considered, and her daughter,
too English by now. But she found the ring,

her mourned and glittering hoop of diamonds,
not lost in a drain after all
but wrenched and twisted into a painful oblong
jammed between the divan-bed and the wall.

CORROSION

It was going to be a novel
about his friend, the seventeen-year-old
with the pale hair; ('younger brother';
that day on the river-bank.)
                              Until
he thought perhaps a sonnet-sequence:
more stripped-down, more crystalline.

Or just one sonnet even, one
imaging of the slight bones
almost visible through that skin,
a fine articulation of golden wire.

The bones were what he most held to,
talking about them often: of how
if David (we could call him)
were to have been drenched with acid
and his skin burnt off, the luminous flesh
burnt, it would make no difference.

The slow acid of age
with its lesser burning
he may also have touched on.

4 MAY 1979

Doom and sunshine stream over the garden.
The mindless daffodils are nodding
bright primped heads at the Tory sky:
such blue elation of spring air!
Such freshness! – the oxides and pollutants
hardly yet more than a sweet dust.
Honesty, that mistaken plant,
has opened several dozen purple buds,
about which the bees are confident.
It might be 1970; it might be 1914.

MADMEN

Odd how the seemingly maddest of men –
sheer loonies, the classically paranoid,
violently possessive about their secrets,
whispered after from corners, terrified
of poison in their coffee, driven frantic
(whether for or against him) by discussion of God,
peculiar, to say the least, about their mothers –
return to their gentle senses in bed.

Suddenly straightforward, they perform
with routine confidence, neither afraid
that their partner will turn and bite their balls off
nor groping under the pillow for a razor-blade;
eccentric only in their conversation,
which rambles on about the meaning of a word
they used in an argument in 1969,
they leave their women grateful, relieved, and bored.

SHAKESPEARE'S HOTSPUR

He gurgled beautifully on television,
playing your death, that Shakespearian actor.
Blood glugged under his tongue, he gagged on
words, as you did. Hotspur, Hotspur:
it was an arrow killed you, not a prince,
not Hal clashing over you in his armour,
stabbing featly for the cameras, and your face
unmaimed. You fell into the hands of Shakespeare,
were given a lovely fluency,
undone, redone, made his creature.
In life you never found it easy
to volley phrases off into the future.
And as for your death-scene, that hot day
at Shrewsbury you lifted your visor:
a random arrow smashed into your eye
and mummed your tongue-tied mouth for ever.

NATURE TABLE

The tadpoles won't keep still in the aquarium;
Ben's tried seven times to count them –
thirty-two, thirty-three, wriggle, wriggle –
all right, he's got better things to do.

Heidi stares into the tank, wearing
a snail on her knuckle like a ring.
She can see purple clouds in the water,
a sky for the tadpoles in their world.

Matthew's drawing a worm. Yesterday
he put one down Elizabeth's neck.
But these are safely locked in the wormery
eating their mud; he's tried that too.

Laura sways with her nose in a daffodil,
drunk on pollen, her eyes tight shut.
The whole inside of her head is filling
with a slow hum of fizzy yellow.

Tom squashes his nose against the window.
He hopes it may look like a snail's belly
to the thrush outside. But is not attacked:
the thrush is happy on the bird-table.

The wind ruffles a chaffinch's crest
and gives the sparrows frilly grey knickers
as they squabble over their seeds and bread.
The sun swings in and out of clouds.

Ben's constructing a wigwam of leaves
for the snails. Heidi whispers to the tadpoles
'Promise you won't start eating each other!'
Matthew's rather hoping they will.

A wash of sun sluices the window,
bleaches Tom's hair blonder, separates
Laura from her daffodil with a sneeze,
and sends the tadpoles briefly frantic;

until the clouds flop down again
grey as wet canvas. The wind quickens,
birds go flying, window-glass rattles,
pellets of hail are among the birdseed.

REVISION

It has to be learned afresh
every new start or every season,
revised like the languages that faltered
after I left school or when I stopped
going every year to Italy. Or
like how to float on my back, swimming,
not swimming, ears full of sea-water;
like the taste of the wine at first communion
(because each communion is the first);
like dancing and how to ride a horse —
can I still? Do I still want to?

The sun is on the leaves again;
birds are making rather special noises;
and I can see for miles and miles
even with my eyes closed.

So yes: teach it to me again.

INFLUENZA

Dreamy with illness
we are Siamese twins
fused at the groin
too languid to stir.

We sprawl transfixed
remote from the day.
The window is open.
The curtain flutters.

Epics of sound-effects
ripple timelessly:
a dog is barking
in vague slow bursts;

cars drone; someone
is felling a tree.
Forests could topple
between the axe-blows.

Draughts idle over
our burning faces
and my fingers over
the drum in your ribs.

You lick my eyelid:
the fever grips us.
We shake in its hands
until it lets go.

Then you gulp cold water
and make of your mouth
a wet cool tunnel.
I slake my lips at it.

CRAB

Late at night we wrench open a crab;
flesh bursts out of its cup

in pastel colours. The dark fronds attract me:
Poison, you say, Dead Men's Fingers –

don't put them in your mouth, stop!
They brush over my tongue, limp and mossy,

until you snatch them from me, as you snatch
yourself, gently, if I come too close.

Here are the permitted parts of the crab,
wholesome on their nests of lettuce

and we are safe again in words.
All day the kitchen will smell of sea.

ECLIPSE

Today the Dog of Heaven swallowed the sun.
Birds twanged for the dusk and fell silent,
one puzzled flock after another –
African egrets; parakeets; Chinese crows.

But firecrackers fended the beast off:
he spat it out, his hot glorious gobful.
Now it will be ours again tomorrow
for the birds here to rediscover at dawn.

What they chirrup to it will ring like praise
from blackbirds, thrushes, eleven kinds of finches,
that certain tribesmen in the south of China
have not unlearnt their pre-republican ways.

ON THE BORDER

Dear posterity, it's 2 a.m.
and I can't sleep for the smothering heat,
or under mosquito nets. The others
are swathed in theirs, humid and sweating,
long white packets on rows of chairs
(no bunks. The building isn't finished).

I prowled in the dark back room for water
and came outside for a cigarette
and a pee in waist-high leafy scrub.
The moon is brilliant: the same moon,
I have to believe, as mine in England
or theirs in the places where I'm not.

Knobbly trees mark the horizon,
black and angular, with no leaves:
blossoming flame-trees; and behind them
soft throbbings come from the village.
Birds or animals croak and howl;
the river rustles; there could be snakes.

I don't care. I am standing here,
posterity, on the face of the earth,
letting the breeze blow up my nightdress,
writing in English, as I do,
in all this tropical non-silence.
Now let me tell you about the elephants.

THE PRIZE-WINNING POEM

It will be typed, of course, and not all in capitals: it will
use upper and lower case
in the normal way; and where a space is usual it will have
a space.
It will probably be on white paper, or possibly blue, but
almost certainly not pink.
It will not be decorated with ornamental scroll-work in
coloured ink,
nor will a photograph of the poet be glued above his or her
name,
and still less a snap of the poet's children frolicking in a
jolly game.
The poem will not be about feeling lonely and being fifteen
and unless the occasion of the competition is a royal
jubilee it will not be about the queen.
It will not be the first poem the author has written in his
life
and will probably not be about the death of his daughter,
son or wife
because although to write such elegies fulfils a therapeutic
need
in large numbers they are deeply depressing for the judges
to read.
The title will not be 'Thoughts' or 'Life' or 'I Wonder
Why'
or 'The Bunny-rabbit's Birthday Party' or 'In Days of
Long Gone By'.
'Tis and 'twas, o'er and e'er, and such poetical
contractions will not be found
in the chosen poem. Similarly clichés will not abound:

dawn will not herald another bright new day, nor dew
                              sparkle like diamonds in a dell,
nor trees their arms upstretch. Also the poet will be able
                              to spell.
Large meaningless concepts will not be viewed with
                              favour: myriad is out;
infinity is becoming suspect; aeons and galaxies are in
                              some doubt.
Archaisms and inversions will not occur; nymphs will not
                              their fate bemoan.
Apart from this there will be no restrictions upon the style
                              or tone.
What is required is simply the masterpiece we'd all write
                              if we could.
There is only one prescription for it: it's got to be good.

AN EMBLEM

Someone has nailed a lucky horse-shoe
beside my door while I was out –
or is it a loop of rubber? No:
it's in two sections. They glide about,
silently undulating: two
slugs in a circle, tail to snout.

The ends link up: it's a shiny quoit
of rippling slug-flesh, thick as a snake,
liquorice-black against the white
paint; a pair of wetly-nak-
ed tubes. It doesn't seem quite right
to watch what kind of love they'll make.

But who could resist? I'll compromise
and give them a little time alone
to nuzzle each other, slide and ooze
into conjunction on their own;
surely they're experts, with such bodies,
each a complete erogenous zone –

self-lubricating, swelling smooth
and boneless under grainy skin.
Ten minutes, then, for them to writhe
in privacy, to slither in-
to position, to arrange each lithe
tapered hose-pipe around its twin.

All right, now, slugs, I'm back; time's up.
And what a pretty coupling I find!
They're swinging from the wall by a rope
of glue, spun out of their combined
mucus and anchored at the top.
It lets them dangle, intertwined,

formally perfect, like some emblem:
heraldic serpents coiled in a twist.
But just in case their pose may seem
immodest or exhibitionist
they've dressed themselves in a cloud of foam,
a frothy veil for love-in-a-mist.

PIANO CONCERTO IN E FLAT MAJOR

In her 1930s bob or even, perhaps,
if she saw something quainter as her fashion,
long thick hair in a plait, the music student
showed her composition to her tutor;
and she aroused, or this enhanced, his passion.

He quoted from it in his new concerto,
offering back to her as homage
those several bars of hers the pianist plays
in the second movement: part of what she dreamed
re-translated, marked more with his image.

But the seven steady notes of the main theme
are his alone. Did the romance go well?
Whether he married her's recorded somewhere
in books. The wistful strings, the determined
percussion, the English cadences, don't tell.

VILLA ISOLA BELLA

'You will find Isola Bella in pokerwork on my heart'
— Katherine Mansfield, to John Middleton Murry,
10 November 1920 (inscribed outside the
Katherine Mansfield memorial room in Menton)

Your villa, Katherine, but not your room,
and not much of your garden. Goods trains boom
all night, a dozen metres from the bed
where tinier tremors hurtle through my head.
The ghost of your hot flat-iron burns my lung;
my throat's all scorching lumps. I grope among
black laurels and the shadowy date-palm, made
like fans of steel, each rustling frond a blade,
across the gravel to the outside loo
whose light won't wake my sleeping sister. You
smoked shameless Turkish all through your TB.
I drag at Silk Cut filters, duty-free,
then gargle sensibly with Oraldene
and spit pink froth. Not blood: it doesn't mean,
like your spat scarlet, that I'll soon be dead –
merely that pharmacists are fond of red.
I'm hardly sick at all. There's just this fuzz
that blurs and syncopates the singing buzz
of crickets, frogs, and traffic in my ears:
a nameless fever, atavistic fears.
Disease is portable: my bare half-week
down here's hatched no maladie exotique;
I brought my tinglings with me, just as you
brought ragged lungs and work you burned to do;
and, as its fuel, your ecstasy-prone heart.
Whatever haunts my bloodstream didn't start
below your villa, in our genteel den
(till lately a pissoir for passing men).
But your harsh breathing and impatient face,
bright with consumption, must have left a trace
held in the air. Well, Katherine, Goodnight:
let's try to sleep. I'm switching out the light.
Watch me through tepid darkness, wavering back
past leaves and stucco and their reverent plaque
to open what was not in fact your door
and find my narrow mattress on the floor.

LANTERN SLIDES

I

'You'll have to put the little girl down.'
Is it a little girl who's bundled
in both our coats against my shoulder,
buried among the trailing cloth?

It's a big haul up to the quay,
my other arm heavy with luggage,
the ship lurching. Who's my burden?
She had a man's voice this morning.

2

Floods everywhere. Monsoon rain
syphoning down into the valley.
When it stops you see the fungus
hugely coiling out of the grass.

Really, in such a derelict lane
you wouldn't expect so many cars,
black and square, driving jerkily.
It's not as if we were near a village.

3

Now here's the bridal procession:
the groom pale and slender in black
and his hair black under his hat-brim;
is that a frock-coat he's wearing?

The bride's as tall as his trouser pocket;
she hoists her arm to hold his hand,
and rucks her veil askew. Don't,
for your peace of mind, look under it.

4

The ceremony will be in a cavern,
a deep deserted underground station
built like a theatre; and so it is:
ochre-painted, proscenium-arched.

119

The men have ribbons on their hatbands;
there they are, behind the grille,
receding with her, minute by minute,
shrivelling down the empty track.

DREAMING

'Oblivion, that's all. I never dream' he said –
proud of it, another immunity,
another removal from the standard frame which she
inhabited, dreaming beside him of a dead
woman tucked neatly into a small bed,
a cot or a child's bunk, unexpectedly.
victim of some friend or lover. 'Comfort me',
said the dreamer, 'I need to be comforted.'
He did that, not bothering to comprehend,
and she returned to her story: a doctor came
to identify the placid corpse in her dream.
It was obscure; but glancing towards the end
she guessed that killer and lover and doctor were the same;
proving that things are ultimately what they seem.

STREET SONG

Pink Lane, Strawberry Lane, Pudding Chare:
someone is waiting, I don't know where;
hiding among the nursery names,
he wants to play peculiar games.

In Leazes Terrace or Leazes Park
someone is loitering in the dark,
feeling the giggles rise in his throat
and fingering something under his coat.

He could be sidling along Forth Lane
to stop some girl from catching her train,
or stalking the grounds of the RVI
to see if a student nurse goes by.

In Belle Grove Terrace or Fountain Row
or Hunter's Road he's raring to go –
unless he's the quiet shape you'll meet
on the cobbles in Back Stowell Street.

Monk Street, Friars Street, Gallowgate
are better avoided when it's late.
Even in Sandhill and the Side
there are shadows where a man could hide.

So don't go lightly along Darn Crook
because the Ripper's been brought to book.
Wear flat shoes, and be ready to run:
remember, sisters, there's more than one.

ACROSS THE MOOR

He had followed her across the moor,
taking shortcuts, light and silent
on the grass where the fair had been –
and in such weather, the clouds dazzling
in a loud warm wind, who'd hear?

He was almost up with her
at the far side, near the road,
when a man with a blotched skin
brought his ugly dogs towards them.
It could have been an interruption.
And as she closed the cattle-gate
in his face almost, he saw
that she was not the one, and let her go.

There had been something. It was
not quite clear yet, he thought.
So he loitered on the bridge,
idle now, the wind in his hair,
gazing over into the stream
of traffic; and for a moment
it seemed to him he saw it there.

BETHAN AND BETHANY

Bethan and Bethany sleep in real linen –
avert your covetous eyes, you starers;
their counterpanes are of handmade lace:
this is a civilized country.

If it is all just one big suburb
gliding behind its freezing mist
it is a decorated one;
it is of brick, and it is tidy.

Above the court-house portico
Justice holds her scales in balance;
the seventeenth-century church is locked
but the plaque outside has been regilded.

Bethan and Bethany, twelve and eleven,
bared their eyes to the television
rose-red-neon-lit, and whispered
in their related languages.

Guess now, through the frilled net curtains,
which belongs here and which doesn't.
Each of them owns the same records;
this is an international culture.

The yobs in the street hoot like all yobs,
hawk and whistle and use no language.
Bethan and Bethany stir in their sleep.
The brindled cat walks on their stomachs.

BLUE GLASS

The underworld of children becomes the overworld
when Janey or Sharon shuts the attic door
on a sunny afternoon and tiptoes in sandals
that softly waffle-print the dusty floor

to the cluttered bed below the skylight,
managing not to sneeze as she lifts
newspapers, boxes, gap-stringed tennis-racquets
and a hamster's cage to the floor, and shifts

the tasselled cover to make a clean surface
and a pillow to be tidy under her head
before she straightens, mouths the dark sentence,
and lays herself out like a mummy on the bed.

Her wrists are crossed. The pads of her fingertips
trace the cold glass emblem where it lies
like a chain of hailstones melting in the dips
above her collarbones. She needs no eyes

to see it: the blue bead necklace, of sapphire
or lapis, or of other words she knows
which might mean blueness: amethyst, azure,
chalcedony can hardly say how it glows.

She stole it. She tells herself that she found it.
It's hers now. It owns her. She slithers among
its globular teeth, skidding on blue pellets.
Ice-beads flare and blossom on her tongue,

turn into flowers, populate the spaces
around and below her. The attic has become
her bluebell wood. Among their sappy grasses
the light-fringed gas-flames of bluebells hum.

They lift her body like a cloud of petals.
High now, floating, this is what she sees:
granular bark six inches from her eyeballs;
the wood of rafters is the wood of trees.

Her breathing moistens the branches' undersides;
the sunlight in an interrupted shaft
warms her legs and lulls her as she rides
on air, a slender and impossible raft

of bones and flesh; and whether it is knowledge
or a limpid innocence on which she feeds
for power hasn't mattered. She turns the necklace
kindly in her fingers, and soothes the beads.

MARY MAGDALENE AND THE BIRDS

1

Tricks and tumbles are my trade; I'm
all birds to all men.
I switch voices, adapt my features,
do whatever turn you fancy.
All that is constant is my hair:

plumage, darlings, beware of it.

2

Blackbird: that's the one to watch –
or he is, with his gloss and weapon.
Not a profession for a female,
his brown shadow. Thrush is better,
cunning rehearser among the leaves,
and speckle-breasted, maculate.

3

A wound of some kind. All that talk
of the pelican, self-wounding,
feeding his brood from an ever-bleeding
bosom turns me slightly sick.

But seriousness can light upon
the flightiest. This tingling ache,
nicer than pain, is a blade-stroke:
not my own, but I let it happen.

4

What is balsam? What is nard?
Sweetnesses from the sweet life,
obsolete, fit only for wasting.

I groom you with this essence. Wash it
down the drain with tears and water.
We are too human. Let it pass.

5

With my body I thee worship:
breast on stone lies the rockdove
cold on that bare nest, cooing
its low call, unlulled,
restless for the calling to cease.

6

Mary Magdalene sang in the garden.
It was a swansong, said the women,
for his downdrift on the river.

It sounded more of the spring curlew
or a dawn sky full of larks,
watery trillings you could drown in.